How to Pray Always
Without Always Praying

How to Pray Always Without Always Praying

SILVIO FITTIPALDI, O.S.A.

Notre Dame, Indiana 46556

Library of Congress Cataloging in Publication Data

Fittipaldi, Silvio E.
How to pray always without always praying.

1. Prayer. I. Title.
BV210.2.F56   248'.3   77-25970
ISBN 0-8190-0623-8

1785

Contents

Preface

Saint Paul has recommended: "Pray always." In our present mechanized, technological society, it would seem that we have forgotten how to pray. Or have we? The reality of prayer is often conceptualized in a very narrow manner. These concepts of prayer in terms of verbal formulas, community worship services, prayer as communication with God, prayer as work often are experienced as inadequate in regard to the "always" of Paul's recommendation. In this book, I do not propose that the above concepts of prayer are incorrect. Rather, it is my purpose to broaden the *concept* of prayer in order that the *reality* of prayer may be more fully recognized.

The thesis on which this book is based is the following: prayer is a human reality; it is grounded in and is a realization of human experiences; these experiences have been formalized in an effort to teach human persons to pray and, hence, to more fully realize their humanity; to realize the reality of the forms of prayer, one must get behind these forms to the experiences of which the forms are an expression and toward which they point. In this way, the "always" of "pray always" may become realizable. Prayer, then, would not be so much something that is done. Rather, prayerfulness would be an orientation in life.

Some human roots of the experience of prayer that will

be discussed are: questioning, wonder, silence, concentration, relatedness, perceptiveness, and grace.

This book, in many ways, is not simply the result of my own experience and reflection. I am deeply indebted to my many friends and teachers who have shared their lives and their questions and their answers with me. While their thinking may rise to the surface on many of the following pages, I take full responsibility for what is said. Furthermore, while I am committed within the Christian tradition, I have been greatly influenced by the other major religious traditions in the world. The following pages are an attempt to articulate an experience of prayer which crosses over the boundaries of the religious traditions as I have assimilated and integrated them into my vision of life.

Finally, I would like to dedicate this book to my parents, Edward and Elvira Fittipaldi who have given me life and continue to support me; and to Rev. John A. Klekotka, O.S.A. who has encouraged me in many ways during the past dozen years, both actively and by his very being.

1

Speaking About Prayer

While in California, on the way to the Orient, a few months before he died, Thomas Merton was asked to speak about prayer. He replied: "Nothing that anyone says will be that important. The great thing is prayer. Prayer itself. If you want a life of prayer, the way to get it is by praying." Merton is saying something very important about the overconceptualization that takes place when prayer is spoken of.

During the last ten years or so of his life, Merton was deeply influenced by the spirituality of the Orient, especially that of Zen. And one of the basic concerns of Zen is with an overintellectualizing of life. In our times when science has offered to people so much for our benefit, an idolization of the scientific method has taken place. This method involves much analysis of data, analysis which means a breaking down of a whole and a thorough investigation of it. At the root of this method, in the popular imagination, is an impeccable logic. It is thought that if something is logical, then it is true. Our language, and hence our speech, is an expression of that logic, which logic is a thing of the mind. In Zen there is a saying: "Not relying on words or letters." This saying is thought to be one dimension of the essence of Zen. It does not deny intellection or language or words or speech, but rather, points to that which is at the root of speech, that which is prior to speech. "Prior" is used here not in a temporal sense, that is, in terms of time, but rather, in what might be called an ontological sense. Shin'ichi Hisamatsu, a contemporary Zen Buddhist, suggests that "not relying on words or letters" is to be "taken to mean 'prior to words' in the sense of not depending on words, not being bound or caught by words."[1] The words point to something beyond themselves.

From a Christian point of view, this is given expression by Jesus in the gospel according to John where he says: "You study the scriptures, believing that in them you have eternal life; now these same scriptures testify to me, and yet you refuse to come to me for life!"[2] While in both the Zen saying and in the saying attributed to Jesus there is no condemnation of speech or words or study or concepts, both point to the root of these articulations. Often we get so wrapped up in our concepts or our language that we forget to live, we forget the very thing about which we are talking. So, too, in speech about prayer, we may become so engrossed in the beautiful descriptions of prayer that we might forget the experience they are attempting to communicate. Thus Merton can say: "If you want a life of prayer, the way to get it is by praying."

A second aspect of Merton's statement is that it points to the inherent limitation of words. When a word is spoken, something is said, but not everything is said. This is deftly pointed out in a story told by a great Chinese sage, Chuang Tzu. Before he tells the story, he discusses the value of books:

> The world values books, and thinks that in so doing it is valuing life. But books contain words only. And yet there is something else which gives value to the books. Not the words only,

not the thought in the words, but something else within the thought, swinging it in a certain direction that words cannot apprehend. But it is the words themselves that the world values when it commits them to books; and though the world values them, these words are worthless as long as that which gives them value is not held in honor. That which man apprehends by observation is only outward form and color, name and noise; and he thinks that this will put him in possession of Life. Form and color, name and sound, do not reach to reality. That is why: "He who knows does not say; he who says, does not know."[3]

An inherent paradox is involved in this saying. I might ask the author or speaker why he even said what he said if "he who says does not know." Is it true then that he does not know, and hence, his words can be doubted? The question is asked: "How then is the world going to know Life through words?" In response, Chuang Tzu tells the following story about Duke Hwan and the wheelwright:

Duke Hwan of Khi, first in his dynasty, sat under his canopy reading his philosophy; and Phien, the wheelwright, was out in the yard making a wheel. Phien laid aside hammer and chisel, climbed the steps, and said to Duke Hwan: "May I ask you, Lord, what is this you are reading? The Duke said: "The experts. The authorities." And Phien asked: "Are they alive or dead?" "Dead a long time," was the reply. "Then," said the wheelwright, "you are reading only the dirt they left behind." Then the Duke replied: "What do you know about it? You are only a wheelwright. You had better give me a good explanation or else you must die." The wheelwright said: "Let us look at the affair from my point of view. When I make wheels, if I go easy, they fall apart; if I am too rough, they do not fit. If I am neither too easy nor too violent, they come out right. The work is what I want it to be. You cannot put this into words; you have to know how it is. I cannot even tell my own son exactly how it is done, and my son cannot learn it from me. So here I am seventy years old, still making wheels! The men of old took all they really knew with them to the grave. And so Lord, what you are reading there is only the dirt they left behind them."[3]

Yet words also have a power to them. Not only do they conceal, they also reveal and in revealing can heal. A word spoken at the right moment, at the right place, to the right person! What power! Thus, there is within the great religious traditions of the world a recognition of the force of words, of speech. This is more evident in Judaism, Christianity, and Islam which are known as religions of the word. The scriptures of these traditions are deeply honored and studied. It is the wise person, however, who not only studies the scriptures, but also lives them. Or better, the scriptures give expression to the life of the wise person. For "the fool says what he knows; the wise man knows what he says," suggests the Hasidic Master, Rabbi Bunam.[4] Or, as Bernard Phillips, one of my teachers once said in class: "The wise man may not know the scriptures. But if they are repeated to him, it is he who can point to their deepest meaning."

The power of speech is not only recognized by the Near-Eastern religions but also by Buddhism. One of the elements of the Buddhist Noble Eightfold Path (an expression of the Enlightenment of the Buddha) is right speech. Right speech does not point exclusively to speaking the truth or not lying, though this is also included. Rather right speech is related speech. Related speech means real communication, which may take place during the dialogue. It does not have to, insofar as the parties may be speaking past each other. Nor is it excluded from a "lecture." Real communication takes place when the words move from heart to heart, from mind to mind, from person to person. The words do not simply come from the one speaking but also from the one being spoken to. This is related speech. A good example of such speech is found in an Hasidic story:

> Every evening after prayer, the Baal-Shem went to his room. Two candles were set in front of him and the mysterious Book of Creation put on the table among other books. Then all those who needed his counsel were admitted in a body, and he spoke with them until the eleventh hour. One evening, when the people left, one of them said to the man beside him how much good the words the Baal-Shem had directed to him, had done him. But the other told him not to talk such nonsense, that they had entered the room together and from that moment on the master had spoken to no one except himself. A third, who heard this, joined in the conversation with a smile, saying how curious that both were mistaken, for the rabbi had carried on an intimate conversation with him the entire evening. Then a fourth and a fifth made the same claim, and finally all began to talk at once and tell what they had experienced. But the next instant they all fell silent.[5]

Related speech is speech which is spoken from the heart of one to another in such a way that it comes from the very heart of the listener, yet it still comes from the one speaking. The speaker really speaks. Why? The speaker knows what is said and says what is known.

St. Paul, in his first letter to the Corinthians, while speaking of the gift of tongues, advises that this gift be for the benefit of the community, that it be related to the members of the community. He asks: "What use shall I be if all my talking reveals nothing new, tells you nothing, and neither inspires you nor instructs you? . . . There are any number of different languages in the world, and not one of them is meaningless, but if I am ignorant of what the sounds mean, I am a savage to the man who is speaking, and he is a savage to me."[6] Paul is concerned with whether or not his speech is related speech.

This, too, can be said about speech about prayer. It is quite limited. It is the dirt that is left behind. It is that which points and should not be confused with that to which it points. Yet, it is also powerful. It does point. And hence, can be healing, enlightening, instructive, and creative. We read in the Book of Genesis: "God *said*, 'Let there be light,' and there was light."[7] And John the Evangelist proclaimed: "In the beginning was the Word: The Word was with God and the Word was God."[8] And this Word can make us free. "If you make my word your home you will indeed be my disciples, you will learn the truth and the truth will make you free."[9]

Our question, then, is not whether or not one can speak about prayer. Rather, the question is: "Who is the one who is speaking?"

The Book of Sirach describes this person in terms of silence and speech:

> There is the man who keeps quiet and is considered wise, another incurs hatred for talking too much.
>
> There is the man who keeps quiet not knowing how to answer, another who keeps quiet, because he knows when to speak.
>
> A wise man will keep quiet till the right moment, but a garrulous fool will always misjudge it.
>
> The man who talks too much will get himself disliked, and the self-appointed oracle will make himself hated.[10]

Words and speech both reveal and conceal. This can happen because of the speaker or because of the hearer.

When the speaker speaks from the heart, the words reveal. But they may not be heard by the hearer. Jesus once said: "Let him who has ears to hear, hear." The hearer must also allow the heart to enter the words of the speaker. On the other hand, the words of the speaker may conceal. They may be words to which the speaker is unrelated. Yet, it might happen that the hearer may hear. The words may speak to the hearer. The heart of the hearer is in the words. Thus to speak about prayer or to read or hear about prayer is to put one's heart into the words. Then the words take on flesh, the flesh of the speaker and/or the hearer.

Speech about prayer, finally, is closely interwoven with one's attitude toward God—who this God is. I do not wish to go into my own beliefs in this matter at any great length (to some extent they will come through what I say of prayer). I simply will give expression to my general approach to God.

The word "God" is the best word we have for saying what we want to say, Karl Rahner suggests in one of his talks, because it tells us nothing.[11] In other words, God is ineffable, the infinite horizon and ultimate depth of life itself. God is mystery. By mystery I do not mean that nothing can be known. Rather, something is known, but we can always know more. We human persons, insofar as we are made in the "image of God" are also mystery, and hence, an imageless image. Thus, I suggest that speech about prayer is speech about God and about the human person, about God as Other and as nearer to us than we are to ourselves, and about the human person as that being who, as Karl Rahner suggests, is "inescapably thrust out of himself into that absolute mystery which is called God" or as "that being which loses itself in God."[12] An "understanding" of God in this manner goes beyond prayer as a communication between God and human persons to prayer as the communion of God and humans. To speak of prayer is to speak of God and to speak of human persons and to speak of their communion. This speech, insofar as it is speech about mystery and possibly speech that arises out of mystery, both reveals and conceals. Something is said, but not everything.

Finally, I would like to suggest that speech about prayer can itself be a prayer. It can be a way of entering into the mystery of God and humans and the world. The speech itself, when it comes from the heart, is a participation in this mystery, a living of this mystery, a being grasped by this mystery.

Notes

1. Shin'ichi Hisamatsu, "Zen: Its Meaning for Modern Civilization," *The Eastern Buddhist*, New Series 1 (September, 1965), p. 23.
2. John 5:39–40.
3. Thomas Merton, *The Way of Chuang Tzu* (New York: New Directions, 1965), p. 82.
4. Martin Buber, *Tales of the Hasidim: The Later Masters* (New York: Schocken, 1948), p. 256.
5. Martin Buber, *Tales of the Hasidim: The Early Masters* (New York: Schocken, 1947), p. 55.
6. 1 Corinthians 14:6, 12.
7. Genesis 1:3.
8. John 1:1.
9. John 8:31–32.

10. Sirach 20:5-8.
11. Karl Rahner, *Grace in Freedom* (New York: Herder and Herder, 1969), p. 185.
12. Karl Rahner, "Christian Humanism," *Journal of Ecumenical Studies* 4, 3 (Summer, 1967), p. 373.

2

Prayer as Questioning

If it is true that God and human persons are mystery, then it follows that more can always be said about the mystery. Hence, anything that is said is open to question. My use of the word "question" in this chapter is not the normal usage. Today a question is usually understood as an intellectual query. I do not wish to exclude this meaning, but rather to broaden it to include "experiential" questions. An "experiential" question is one which is asked with one's mind and heart, body and feelings, wonderings and longings. It is a question spoken not only in word but also in one's eyes and hands, ears and feet. It is a question that may be articulated, yet is very often unable to be spoken. It is the question that is contained in expectation and anticipation, in fear and in terror, in love and in hate.

Some examples may help in understanding what I mean by an "experiential" question. Imagine that someone has said to you: "I want to see you." Your mind begins to operate, wondering what the meeting is for. Emotions of fear, maybe, or even joyful expectation arise, depending on the questioner and your relationship with that person. What question is being asked? It is : "Why do you want to see me?" The question is not necessarily spoken. Nor is it simply mental? It is also felt.

Other examples are:

"Can I trust you?" or

"Why should I get up this morning?" or

"Why don't I trust you?" or

"Can I open myself to this person?" or

"What will I do with my life?" or

"Can I keep living this way without destroying myself?" or

"Will I be able to fulfill this responsibility?" or

"What must I do—here—now?" or

"Will I be able to get to sleep tonight?"

These questions are not only intellectual, they are physical, emotional, and intellectual. They are also asked by different people in many different ways. They are asked by the same person in a variety of ways. Nor are they the only questions. I am sure the reader can add many more. Nor do our questions concern only ourselves. Other questions that are asked may concern other people whose lives are tied to our own, or even refer to people who are strangers. Thus it might be asked:

"Will this child ever grow up and be independent?"

"Why does this elderly grandmother (or grandfather) have to suffer so much?"

At two a.m., a child coughing: "Will she ever stop coughing?"

"When will this baby stop crying?"

"What can I do to enable this child to grow?"

Doctor Teague Summer, a central character in the powerfully sensitive novel by Marilyn Harris, *Hatter Fox,* is a man whose life had become a living question. Summer had been called to a Sante Fe jail to care for a wounded young man. In the same cell as that young man were twenty other inmates, male and female. Summer was attacked by one of these people, Hatter Fox, and stabbed in the back. During the following weeks Summer was haunted by her, and he was strangely drawn to her. He wondered why. He went to see her. While viewing her almost lifeless body and spirit in the cell, he cried out to himself:

> Why? Why everything? Why the need for such a room? Why the need for emergency calls to jail cells where kids have cut their wrists? Why Hatter Fox? Why the human waste beyond redemption, beyond help? And finally, why in the hell was I standing there, apparently transfixed by a young girl who had tried to kill me?[1]

Summer was questioning the situation as many people might question their own personal situation or question a particular condition made evident by a news report. Summer was also questioning himself. He felt that he was a second-rate doctor. He had no interest, as such, in Hatter nor in her people, the Navahos. Yet, here he was in her cell. And a few days later, he would be driving to a reformatory in Albuquerque to be consulted in regard to Hatter. Summer's mind continued to spin, trying to make sense of his actions. He imagined himself as an "army-surplus Don Quixote." He felt he was a "sucker." And, finally, he could not imagine himself as anyone or anything. Hatter, it seemed, had become for him a symbol of all his past failures. These are the questions that drove this one man, questions about himself, about others and about the particular conditions in a particular place in the world. It is these questions that he lives and embodies throughout the novel. Thomas Merton gives expression to Summer's kind of questions and hence to the questioning prayer of which I am speaking when he writes in his book *Contemplative Prayer:*

> But underlying all life is the ground of doubt and self-

questioning which sooner or later must bring us face to face with the ultimate meaning of our life. This self-questioning can never be without a certain existential "dread"—a sense of insecurity, of "lostness," of exile, of sin. A sense that one has somehow been untrue not so much to abstract moral or social norms but to one's own inmost truth.[2]

Summer was confronting his past failures, trying to free himself, not from their reality, but from their power to define him. He was in search of his own inmost truth.

What do these questions have to do with prayer? I hope to show that they have everything to do with prayer. Elie Wiesel, in his personal memoir *Night,* asks the question: "Why did I pray?" He received a response from his teacher Moshe, who said:

> Man raises himself toward God by the questions he asks him. . . . That is true dialogue. Man questions God and God answers. But we don't understand his answers. We can't understand them, because they come from the depths of the soul, and they stay there until death. . . . I pray to the God within me that he will give me the strength to ask him the right questions.[3]

But what does God have to do with the questions that I raised above? I was not even thinking of God. The questions were a simple cry arising out of a situation. They are totally human. What does God have to do with the questions of Teague Summer? They do not refer to God at all. How can these questions raise a person to God, as Wiesel suggests? Why even want to be raised to God?

A response to these questions (and it is not an answer) is that a question asked is an opening of one's self to something "other" than the usual, and even "other" than oneself. To ask a question is to realize that I have some input into that very situation in which the question is posed. For example, a child gets hit in the mouth by a hockey stick. The situation is established. All my plans for the next few hours, or perhaps for the rest of the day or even for a few days, will have to be changed. I respond to the child. I am putting some input into the situation. It changes the situation a little. I have been open to something other than I had planned. I have also responded and entered into that otherness. In every question, "otherness" enters into the life of the questioner. This is what it means to live life as mystery. It is an openness to unexpected otherness. But it is also the attempt to live with expected otherness, for example, to live with people who are known to be very different. This is how a person is raised toward God by the questions that are asked. The person becomes open to otherness and responds to that otherness.

However, God is not only present in the questions because the questions are openings to otherness. Questions are also expressions of a search into the depth of reality. Dr. Summer, in *Hatter Fox,* questioned himself and his situation and these questions lead him deeper into the depths. The deeper he went, the closer to mystery he came, the nearer to himself and his situation. He was led to be nearer to himself than he had ever been. As a person approaches that mystery of himself or herself, God is approached. Questions not only are an opening to otherness. A person is raised to God by the questions he or she asks by continuously encountering otherness as well as the depths of nearness. God is totally other yet nearer to us than we are to ourselves.

The questions that are asked are not only for the sake of conversation or to make an impression. They are, rather, questions which arise from the living experience of the questioner. Wiesel did not ask: "What is prayer?" He asked: "Why did I pray?" The response of Moshe was that he prayed because of the questions that he asked, that these questions were the springboard by which he could raise himself up to God.

These very questions themselves are a prayer. It is this searching questioning that Merton describes as characteristic of religious meditation. He suggests that the *search* for truth which springs from a relationship of love is a distinctive characteristic of religious meditation. It is this grounding in love that makes our *quest* (notice that this word has the same root as the word "question") for truth a prayer which shatters the dark clouds that stand between us and God.[4] The truth that is sought here is that contained, as it were, in the question I asked above. Religious meditation is not the norm. Rather, it itself is imitative of the human situation of questioning. Religious meditation is a formal way of trying to do what we can do each day in each situation. It is also a discipline by which we can become trained to ask these everyday questions with our whole selves. It is thus that questioning is "primitive" prayer. I do not mean "primitive" to mean immature. Rather, "primitive" is descriptive of something primary or basic—one's situation in life.

Wiesel also said that the questions would be answered but that we would not understand the answers. In one of his novels, Wiesel takes this observation a little further. He is still searching for an answer. Wiesel is a Jew. He had lived through a Nazi concentration camp. The experience shattered him. He wrote:

> Once, in the Orient, I talked of suicide with a sage whose clear and gentle eyes seemed forever to be gazing at a never-ending

sunset. "Dying is no solution," he affirmed. "And living?" I
asked. "Nor living either," he conceded. "But who tells you
there is a solution?"

You will not convince me he was not right. He was too wise not
to realize that one can do without solutions. Only the questions matter. We may share them or turn away from them.
Either way, you will in the end admit they hold no answers.
Only secrets.[5]

Many continue to seek solutions. Is God the solution? Is
God the answer to my questions? To respond to this question positively may have many meanings. It might mean
that I can see no light anywhere and have to believe there
is some answer or I can't keep going. It may be a cop-out
where God becomes the solution to unsolved questions,
where God fills up the blanks in our knowledge. Or, it
might merely mean that the answer is not yet evident, yet I
trust that I will someday, somehow find an answer. Is Jesus
the answer? The same can be said for Jesus as for God.
Then is love the answer? Wiesel responds to this question
and in his response might give a response to whether or not
God is the answer. He writes: "Do you understand now that
love, no matter how personal or universal, is not a solution?
And that outside of love there is no solution."[6] Love does
not tell me what I must do. Questions arise and are answered in a dialogue of love. More questions arise from the
answers, and so on. I am reminded here of the delightful
Sufi tale concerning Nasrudin. One day Nasrudin was
asked: "Why do you always answer a question with another
question?" Immediately, Nasrudin responded: "Do I?"[7]

To have a question answered by another question which
itself is answered by a further question can become somewhat unnerving. This path is not the easiest way. Wiesel is

very aware of this. In his novel *The Town Beyond the Wall,* he writes:

> It isn't easy to live always under a question mark. But who says that the essential question has an answer? The essence of man is to be a question, and the essence of the question is to be without answer.[8]

To live under a question, especially one without answer is truly not an easy path to follow. The difficulty is also evident in the Hindu Jnana Yoga, the Way of Knowledge. Among the Hindus, the Way of Knowledge is the path to liberation for those who have a strong "intellectual" bent. It is the shortest path, but also the steepest. The spirit of this way is expressed by the Jewish prophet Jeremiah, who placed the following words on the tongue of Yahweh:

> When you call to me and come to plead with me, I will listen to you. When you seek me you shall find me, when you seek me with all your heart, I will let you find me.[9]

The way is called the Way of Knowledge, but the "knowledge" is the knowledge of the heart, where "heart" symbolizes the core of a person. This is the way of pleading and seeking, the way of questioning. It is further illustrated by a story told to me by Bernard Phillips. A Hindu guru and his disciple were traveling from village to village. They walked for several hours during which time they were in deep conversation concerning fundamental questions of life and God. They came upon a river. The guru stopped, guided his disciple to the river and proceeded to hold the disciple's head under the water. He held it there until the disciple began to shake from the inability to breath. His whole body was calling out for air. Finally, the guru allowed the disciple to come up for air. Raising his head out of the water, the disciple gasped for his breath, for his life. When he finally became calm, he asked his guru, why? The guru responded: "When you want God as much as you wanted air, you will have him." The way of questioning is certainly not an easy way, especially if the questioner cannot even expect an answer to the question. But we can also ask if there is really a question if there is no answer.

A few years ago, I was asked by a friend what it meant to be human. The only response I could think of at the time was: "The fact that you ask that question is what it means to be human." I would add now that that is what it means to pray, that is, to go below the surface of life, to live from one's depths, yet never rejecting the surface, but by the very fact of plumbing the depth, one can really live on the surface.

This kind of living takes trust, a trust that can be expressed in questions which attempt to enter the mystery which we call life, the mystery which arises from another person, the mystery which calls to us from out of particular situations. To ask a question is to trust that there may be a response. To ask a question is to open oneself, and hence, to become vulnerable. The trust is not necessarily easy. It may come forth in fear and trembling as the question of a mother and father who wonder about whether or not their young child will be able to live happily or even to simply make a decent life in this world. Or, the question of a parent who wonders if he or she will have the energy to raise their physically disabled or emotionally disturbed child. Such an enterprise requires trust. It is this trust that is present in a question. The very ground of questioning is trust. There is, however, some untrust in a question. A question can arise because of a kind of itch, an itch that all

is not as it can be. If all is not as it can be, there is some
mistrust of the present condition. To merely trust in this
situation would mean to leave it as it is. Not to trust it is to
want it changed. Thus, a question contains a degree of
trust that the condition can change and also a mistrust of
the present condition which mistrust is a catalyst for a
possible change. Prayer as this kind of questioning is
grounded is trust which also has an element of mistrust.

The method of questioning is deeply imbedded in the traditional training of the Zen postulant. When the postulant
seeks admittance to a monastery, he or she is refused at first,
and left to wait and continue seeking admission. Upon admission, the postulant begins the training, which is the *mondo* (question and answer). The *mondo* is one of the most
characteristic features of Zen methodology of teaching.
This *mondo* takes place between a master and the disciple.
It is the master's attempt to get the disciple to face self in
all its nakedness so that enlightenment might ensue. It is
the master's attempt to get the student to become the question. For, as D. T. Suzuki suggests:

> So long as the Buddha had his question before him, so long as
> he had it outside and separate from himself, as if it could be
> solved by external means, it could never be solved. The ques-
> tion comes out of the questioner. But when it is out, the ques-
> tioner mistakenly thinks it is something outside himself. The
> question is answered only when it is identified with the ques-
> tioner.[10]

This observation by Suzuki can be illustrated by a story.
There was a man who came to study under a Zen master
and spent some three years of hard work in his attempt to
attain enlightenment. The time was growing short until he
would have to return home, so he approached the master

and told him of his predicament. The master asked him to stay for two more weeks and at the end of that time, the disciple was promised, he would be enlightened. This was done and the state of the man was the same. He again approached the master who gave him another two weeks. The result was the same. The time was then reduced to five days and then to three days. The disciple was becoming anxious. He had worked hard and there were no results. He had to go home. Still, no enlightenment. Finally, the master said to him: "Stay for three more days. If you are not enlightened by the end of that time, you will die." Within those three days the disciple was enlightened. The question was no longer outside him. He was the question.

Unless one might get the impression that the Zen *mondo* training is to be found only in a Zen monastery where one encounters a human master, I will suggest that, for most people who will never meet a "master," the *mondo* are provided by life itself. If our eyes and ears are open, we do not have to look beyond our own doorstep for questions. Then we could again apply Suzuki's comment: "The question is answered only when it is identified with the questioner."

The Christian gospels are also sprinkled with these *mondo* type exchanges between Jesus and his disciples or between Jesus and the leaders of the people. Since there are too many to mention all here, I will point to only two. We are all familiar with the encounter between Jesus and the Jewish doctors of the Law. At the age of twelve, when his parents took him to Jerusalem for the feast of the Passover, Jesus remained behind. When his parents found him, "he was sitting among the doctors, listening to them, and asking them questions." When Jesus was discovered, Joseph and Mary were overcome and Mary asked him: "My child, why have you done this to us? See how worried your father and I have been, looking for you." And Jesus' reply was even more significant than the fact that he was sitting and questioning the doctors of the Law. He responded to his parents with two further questions: "Why were you looking for me? Did you not know that I must be busy with my Father's affairs?"[11] This story is filled with questions. Most emphasis is usually given to the questions of Jesus, his questioning of the doctors of the Law and his questions to his parents. Yet there are times when I am more deeply touched by the profoundly human question of Mary, the question that forced her to retrace her steps to seek her only son who was lost, the question that came out of her body and mind and feelings, the question that was of her heart. Mary had truly become her question. It was her prayer.

A second example is from the gospel according to John.[12] This passage describes the encounter between Jesus and the Samaritan woman at the well. This woman had persisted with her questions to Jesus whom she recognized as a prophet. Her series of questions and the responses given to her led to faith on the part of herself and the people of her village. Their prayer was heard. For they became the question and hence became their prayer. The *mondo* is not only a method for teaching how to pray. The *mondo* itself is the prayer. This incident also manifests that questions not only give expression to a hidden dimension of a person or the world, but also that questions can be revelatory. When a person becomes their question, that person becomes open to unknown responses. The response, when it comes (if it does come), may reveal to the person an aspect of their being never dreamed of.

It is of the essence of a human person to be a question and each person is made in the "image of God." Then

God, too, is a question. The "image of God" as a question is quite prominent in the prophet Hosea. The relationship of Israel to their God is portrayed as the relationship between wife and husband. The wife leaves her husband and is unfaithful. The husband wonders what to do and decides to lure her back to himself. He pursues her to lead her out of the wilderness. He speaks to her heart. The God of Israel is in pursuit of his people. He touches their heart and they pursue him. The God of Israel pursues himself as his people pursue him. His passion becomes their passion. His question becomes their question. His quest becomes their quest. His prayer becomes their prayer. God is the question of "Man," *as* "Man" is the question of God. God is the question of "Man" *because* "Man" is the question of God. And so we read in Psalm 42:

As a doe longs for running streams,
so longs my soul for you, my God.

My soul thirsts for God, the God of life;
when shall I go to see the face of God?[13]

This longing for God is often expressed in the form of a contention. The innocent Job cries out from his sadness. He curses the day of his birth:

Why did I not die new-born,
not perish as I left the womb?[14]

Job vacillates between trust and fear:

Oh may my prayer find fulfillment,
may God grant me hope! ...

But have I the strength to go on waiting?
What use is life to me,

when doomed to certain death?
Is mine the strength of stone,
or is my flesh bronze?
Can any power be found within myself,
has not all help deserted me?[15]

Job cried out to his God. He feels himself alone and deserted. His cry is his question. It wracks his spirit and his body. He is his question.

The poet of the psalms also cries out in his anguish:

Forever? How much longer will you hide your face from me?
How much longer must I endure grief in my soul, and sorrow
in my heart by day and by night?[16]

In Psalm 88, the lament becomes even stronger and more detailed:

I call for help all day, I weep to you all night, Yahweh, my
God.[17]

The psalmist is alone, forgotten, cast to the depths of darkness, repulsive to his friends. His God is absent from him. He is absent from his God.

Nor is Jesus excused from such anguish, from such cries. In the garden called Gethsemane, he prays: "My father, if it is possible, let this cup pass me by."[18] And "in his anguish he prayed even more earnestly, and his sweat fell to the ground like great drops of blood."[19] His question is spoken with his entire being. But another element enters, an element that is not lacking in Job or in the psalms. This is the deep trust in God expressed by Jesus when he says: "Nevertheless, let it be as you, not I, would have it."[20] The foundation of the questioning is a deep-felt and known trust. Yet, there is also uncertainty. There is the question.

This faith and openness is also manifest in Mary who asked: "How can this come about, since I am a virgin?"[21] It is the faith of a Martha who protested: "If you had been here, my brother would not have died, but I know that even now, whatever you ask of God, he will grant you."[22] There is an Hasidic story which deftly illustrates this relationship between faith and questioning. It is called *The Fiftieth Gate:*

> Without telling his teacher anything of what he was doing, a disciple of Rabbi Barukh's had inquired into the nature of God, and in his thinking had penetrated further and further until he was tangled in doubts, and what had been certain up to this time, became uncertain. When Rabbi Barukh noticed that the young man no longer came to see him as usual, he went to the city where he lived, entered his room unexpectedly, and said to him: "I know what is hidden in your heart. You have passed through the fifty gates of reason. You begin with a question and think, and think up an answer—and the first gate opens, and to a new question! And again you plumb it, find the solution, fling open the second gate—and look into a new question. On and on like this, deeper and deeper, until you have forced open the fiftieth gate. There you stare at a question whose answer no man has ever found, for if there were one who knew it, there would no longer be freedom of choice. But if you dare to probe further, you plunge into the abyss." "So I should go back all the way, to the very beginning," cried the disciple. "If you turn, you will not be going back," said Rabbi Barukh. "You will be standing beyond the last gate; you will stand in faith."[23]

The disciple will not deny his questioning. He will simply stand in a different place. His question will not be answered. He will simply stand in faith, the faith not of a beginner, but the faith of a man who has crossed the river and now must continue his journey.

It is because of this—that is, that "Man" is the question of God—that Matthew can say: "Your Father knows what you need before you ask him."[24] The questioner becomes the question. The pray-er becomes the prayer. "Ask and it will be given you; search, and you will find; knock and the door will be opened to you. For the one who asks always receives; the one who searches always finds; the one who knocks will always have the door opened to him."[25] The searching is the finding, the knocking is the opening. This asking is founded on faith, as expressed in the gospel according to John: "If you remain in me and my words remain in you, you may ask what you will and you shall get it."[26]

Finally, a very profound question that many of us ask either consciously or unconsciously is uttered by Rabbi Levi Yitzhak. His question does not arise at a special moment or because of an unusual happening. His question is one that can be asked by any person at anytime anywhere. What did Levi Yitzhak ask? He cried out to his God that he was not interested in the secret of the divine ways. He murmured:

> But show me one thing; show it to me more clearly and deeply; show me what this very moment, what is happening at this very moment, means to me, what it demands of me, what you, Lord of the World, are telling me by way of it.[27]

Prayer, then, is a question, God's question addressed to us and our questions addressed to God. Prayer is just as much the questions we pose to life and those by which life challenges us. These questions are transparent in our day to day wonderings and wanderings, expectations and longings, fears and tremblings, demands and periods of quiet. The questions arise out of the depth of life and also from its surface. They are grounded in a trust which does not deny or forego the questions, but now asks them from the heart.

Notes

1. Marilyn Harris, *Hatter Fox* (New York: Bantam, 1974), pp. 8-9.
2. Thomas Merton, *Contemplative Prayer* (New York: Herder and Herder, 1969), p. 26.
3. Elie Wiesel, *Night* (New York: Avon, 1969), pp. 13-14.
4. Thomas P. McDonnell, ed., *A Thomas Merton Reader* (New York: Harcourt, Brace and World, 1962), p. 373.
5. Elie Wiesel. *A Beggar in Jerusalem* (New York: Avon, 1971), pp 15-16,
6. Ibid., p. 172.
7. Idries Shah, *The Pleasantries of the Incredible Mulla Nasrudin* (New York: Dutton, 1971), p. 87.
8. Elie Wiesel, *The Town Beyond the Wall* (New York: Avon, 1969), p. 187.
9. Jeremiah 29:12-14.
10. D. T. Suzuki, *The Field of Zen* (New York: Perennial Library, 1970), p. 15.
11. Luke 2:41-50.
12. John 4:5-42.
13. Psalm 42:1-2.
14. Job 3:11.
15. Job 6:8, 11-13.
16. Psalm 13:1-2.
17. Psalm 88:1.
18. Matthew 26:39.
19. Luke 22:44.

20. Matthew 26:39.
21. Luke 1:24.
22. John 11:21.
23. Martin Buber, *Tales of the Hasidim: The Early Masters* (New York: Schocken, 1947), p. 92.
24. Matthew 6:8.
25. Matthew 7:7–8.
26. John 15:7.
27. Buber, *Tales of the Hasidim: Early Masters,* pp. 212–213.

3

Prayer as Wonder

Insofar as prayer is a radical questioning, a questioning at the root of life, a questioning which arises from the very situation of life, it also involves a sense of wonder. Often, when we question, we say: "I wonder." As we saw above, questioning involves an openness to mystery in life. Wonder is a vibrant entry into that mystery.

Saint-Exupery's Little Prince is a wondering person. He asked many questions, gentle questions, wondering questions. As his friend the pilot, for example, described an airplane to him, the Prince cried out, "What! You dropped from the sky?" His question contains an element of "unbelief," and an element of wonder.[1] The Prince was also a lover of sunsets. One day, on one small planet, he saw the sunset forty-four times. He wondered. Yet he was also sad: "One loves the sunset, when one is so sad," he mused. Wonder is not only joyful. It can also be sad. The Prince also had great difficulty with adults who were always involved with "matters of consequence." Their wonder was restricted to what is important. The Prince did not deny importance to those matters. He simply extended importance to simple things like mushrooms and roses and sheep and hats and elephants. His wonder was inclusive, rather than exclusive. The Little Prince is open to the mystery, to what he sees and what he doesn't see. He is a wondering person.

The Little Prince embodies three senses of the experience of wonder which I will develop in the following
pages. The first two are quite similar to each other. They
both pertain directly to questioning. There is curiosity
which has the flavor of active seeking and there is a questioning which is more subtle than curiosity, which I will call
a gentle questioning. This latter is expressed in the soft,
gentle, reflective murmur: "I wonder." Finally, wonder is
an exclamation which is expressive of marvel.

While it may have some leanings toward the future,
wonder is a very present experience. It is experienced in
that one moment when the ocean is striking in its vastness
and greenness and movement and power and gentleness.
It is the marvel that a conversation has taken place or that
there can really be a relationship with this particular person. It is the feeling that spring has finally come after a
long winter. It is contained in the exclamation; "I can be
alive, I can breathe, I can see, I can feel the wind on my
body." It is the realization that there is laughter, creativity,
rest, endings, beginnings, insight. It is the feeling and
realization that something has finally gone well. It is the
joy of openness to the world, to nature, to other human
persons. Wonder, in fact, can be experienced as a "mini-
vacation" in the midst of labor and pain and striving.
Wonder is the joy of questioning. It is the curious seeking
that is totally self-engaging such that one is really unself-
conscious, yet very involved in the relationship that is present at the moment. These experiences tell us something
about prayer. They are integral to prayer. I would go so
far as to say that they are prayer.

Such wonder or marvel is often expressed in Japanese
haiku poetry. The haiku "captures" the wonder of a moment insofar as the author is fully present in that particular place at that specific moment. A person "sees" a flower.

Both person and flower are transparent. This transparency is evident in the well-known haiku by Basho:

When I look carefully
I see the nazuna blooming
By the hedge![2]

The "capture" is paradoxical insofar as the haiku does not merely "hold" the moment but also frees it by noticing it in wonder. Another good example is to be found in a poetic comment on one of my favorite haiku poems, "On Basho's Frog:"

Under the cloudy cliff, near the temple door,
Between dusky spring plants on the pond,
A frog jumps in the water, plop!
Startled, the poet drops his brush.[3]

The power of wonder can be blocked. In the gospel according to Luke, we read of an encounter between Jesus and his disciples. The disciples were arguing among themselves as to which one was the greatest. This argument portrayed a group of men who felt they had the answer and who were very self-conscious. No one of them was curious about what the other felt or knew.[4] They were arguing over relative position or status. This kind of argument rules out curiosity. The authority is the one with the highest position. There are many times when we have heard or used this argument from authority. It usually cuts off the discussion very quickly and can weaken the spirit of curiosity and, hence, deaden wonder.

In the gospel according to Matthew, Jesus is approached by his disciples with the question: "Who is the greatest in the kingdom of heaven?" Jesus responded by calling a little child to himself and saying: "I tell you solemnly, unless you change and become like little children, you will never enter the kingdom of heaven. And so, the one who makes himself as little as this little child is the greatest in the kingdom of heaven."[5] One way of understanding this elusive passage is that Jesus is referring to the child's openness, to the child's sense of curiosity. The child does not believe that he or she has all the answers. The child can wonder. A child has not yet developed an authority complex as the disciples in the passage referred to above. Who is the greatest? The one who can wonder, who can seek, and who can be curious. Sometimes I feel it is a wonder even to meet a wondering person, child or adult.

Wonder also involves a sense of longing. There is an element of future here but it is not prominent. On the surface, longing may seem to be a "wanting-something-to-happen" which seems almost impossible. Longing, however, arises out of a mood which is very present, a present sense of limitation with a strong sense of something "more" which goes beyond the question of whether or not the "more" is possible. This is closely related to but not the same as "expectation." During the past summer a friend provided me with some understanding of this kind of longing. The day had been overcast. Clouds hid the sun. A mist filtered its rays. It had been this way for a few weeks. There had been moments when the sunlight had broken between the clouds. But these moments were few, were brief and often missed. My friend longed for the sun. A day could be more than it has been. When? The question is a strong, gentle, wondering question.

Again, it would seem that expectation is very future oriented. This future is not isolated, however, from the past or from the present. The past is not all there is, nor is the present. But better, to expect is to see into the present in its fullness. Maurice Friedman speaks of hope in this way, as the pregnancy of the present. There is more to the present than meets the eye. And when it does meet the eye, that present becomes *wonder*-full. It is here that visions (seeings) are born.

There is a passage in the Book of Isaiah and another in the Book of Revelation which give expression to the wonder of which I have spoken above. The authors of these passages are not given to naive, idealistic dreams of the future. Both have done a lot of living in situations which are very painful. They cry out from these situations and their cry is a cry of wonder and longing. In Isaiah we read:

> I shall rejoice over Jerusalem and exult in my people. No more will the sound of weeping or the sound of cries be heard in her. . . . To die at the age of a hundred will be dying young; not to live to be a hundred will be a sign of a curse. They will build houses and inhabit them, plant vineyards and eat their fruit. They will not build for others to live in, or plant so others can eat. For my people shall live as long as trees, and my chosen ones wear out what their hands have made. They will not toil in vain or beget children to their own ruin . . . Long before they call I shall answer; before they stop speaking I shall have heard.[6]

The author of the Book of Revelation almost repeats what is wondered by Isaiah. While speaking of a New Jerusalem, of a new heaven and a new earth, he writes:

> Here God lives among men. He will make his home among them; they shall be his people, and he will be their God; his name is God-with-them. He will wipe away all their tears from their eyes; there will be no more death, and no more mourning or sadness. The world of the past has gone.[7]

Imagine—no one dies, no more tears, living as long as trees, not begetting children to their own ruin! This is not a vision of a future utopia. They are flights of imaginative wonder in which is expressed a profound compassion. They are a few brief moments when the pain has been eased. Passages like this are not confined to people who lived thousands of years ago. They are found even among our contemporaries. Even a man like Daniel Berrigan who is deeply aware of the inhumanity in our world and who spent months in prison could exclaim:

> I hope (imagine!) no one dies. No one dies. I mean the final glacial death—into hopelessness, into violence, into power that is empty of conscience, into dread and nausea and inaction and egoism and base fear.[8]

Imagine, just imagine, Berrigan can still wonder and from that wonder arises a vision, not of the future merely, but of the present and its pregnancy.

Hatter Fox is a fictional character who also can still wonder. In a previous chapter we met Dr. Teague Summer, the doctor who was haunted by Hatter, and we listened to some of his questions. In the eyes of most people Hatter was a social deviant who should have been locked up and the key thrown away. Summer, however, stayed with her defiance and rejection of him and society and, in time, she began to open to him. What did Summer see? He saw a young woman who had lived as a child in many homes, a child who was abused by everyone, a young girl who, at times, supported herself by being a fraternity prostitute. Hatter was bitter and angry and defiant. It would seem that she could not wonder. Yet, as Summer was to discover, deep in her soul, heavily guarded and protected, was a gentle vision of natural beauty. This vision, however, did break through her protective walls on a quiet afternoon during which she and Summer were in the hills near

Albuquerque. Hatter's vision is a challenge to us, yet it also expresses her own hidden but still present ability to wonder. Speaking of Albuquerque, she says:

> I wish they would go away and let the fields have it back. Let the fields and the canyons and the mountains have it all back, the empty space beneath the sky. Clear all that away, send the people packing back to where they came from. Let the fields and sky and mountains fill the empty space until it isn't empty any longer.[9]

Not only is there wonder is this vision of a "virgin wilderness," but there is also a deep sadness. Sadness and wonder are not inconsistent. Such sadness is expressed by Hatter as she recognizes the impossibility of her vision, but her question at the time also contains another sad wonder. She asks: "Summer, do you ever feel like nothing in the world is ever going to be the way it should be?"[10]

In general, weeping can be expressive of a variety of feelings and experiences. It can be painful and it can be wonderous. Weeping can express suffering, the pain of "too much" or the tears of "not enough." Weeping can also give expression to a person's discovery of a way to deal with their pain. The painful weeping may contain the tears of an empty vision, the feeling that there is no way out. The joyful weeping may contain the tears of a fulfilled vision, the feeling that there is a way open. Here the tears of joy arose out of the tears of agony. There tears of agony remain only that. Isaiah and the author of the Book of Revelation speak of and to both these kinds of weeping. To the first, the painful tears, they simply describe their pain, and they know that someone affirms them in their pain without denying their pain or denying their helpless feeling. This response itself is a wonder. It can engender:

"Someone knows my condition and does not belittle it."
For the persons of joyful tears, these sages describe their
condition and then give expression to their vision. And
this too is wonderful!

While all this seems to be irrational and out of the ordinary, it arises out of the depths of the ordinary. It contains
the unreasonable wonder expressed in the words of Jesus:
"The kingdom of heaven is close at hand."[11]

There is a fascination here, which, as Rudolf Otto points
out, is an element of the experience of the holy. Fascination is the opposite of indifference. To be indifferent is to
withold oneself and one's attention. It is to view everyone
and everything in the same manner. Indifference is
passionlessness. To be fascinated, however, is to feel deeply and to be attentive and to relish the uniqueness of a
person or place or thing or moment. To be fascinated is to
be grasped, held, and caught in fear and trembling as well
as in trust and confidence. It is to pray with Paul:

> This, then, is what I pray, kneeling before the Father, from
> whom every family, whether spiritual or natural, takes its
> name. Out of his infinite glory may he give you the power
> through his Spirit for your hidden self to grow strong, so that
> Christ may live in your hearts through faith, and then,
> planted in love and built on love, you will with all the saints
> have strength to grasp the breadth and the length, the height
> and the depth; until knowing the love of Christ, which is
> beyond all knowledge, you are filled with the utter fullness of
> God.[12]

The praying person wonders, is caught in the present by
the subject of his or her wonder in such a way that he or
she is confident in the wonder and questioning, trustful in
the searchings. Or, to put this a bit more mildly—he or she
can keep going and yet cry out in the spirit of Paul that

"eye has not seen, or ear heard, nor has it entered into the heart of man, what things God has prepared for those that love him."[13]

These brief moments of wonder can give courage and strength to act or to be quiet. It is like the man who found a treasure hidden in a field and for sheer joy went and sold all he had to buy that field. The point here is not that he sold all he had to buy the field, but rather, that he was caught up in his wonder, went beyond himself and could extend himself in action.[14]

Wonder can also produce the energy by which a person can dedicate his or her life to a certain pursuit. Such is the experience of Pierre Teilhard de Chardin. Stories are told of how he wept when he saw a human hair consumed by the flames in the hearth of his childhood home; or of how he sought through the fields and roads and woods for anything durable such as rocks or bits of crystal; and finally, how, at the age of six, he exclaimed with wonder and admiration when he came upon a piece of iron from an old plough: "My iron—my divine iron."[15] This wonder at the things of the earth never left Teilhard. He was caught by it and freed by it. Such wonder invigorated Teilhard's lifelong search for the innerness of matter. He was able to say in *The Divine Milieu,* after speaking of the burden of matter that:

> Matter is physical exuberance, ennobling contact, virile effort and the joy of growth. It attracts, renews, unites and flowers. By matter we are nourished, lifted up, linked to everything else, invaded by life. To be deprived of it is intolerable.... Who will give us an immortal body?[16]

It is in the light and strength and energy of such a wonder that Teilhard lived his life with sensitivity and courage.

The joy of wonder is also magnificently expressed in the

dancing of the Hasid. It is a moment of joy that enters briefly into the hardness of daily life. It is told of the dancing of
one rabbi:

> His foot was as light as that of a four-year-old child. And
> among all who saw his holy dancing, there was not one in whom
> the holy turning was not accomplished, for in the hearts of all
> who saw he worked both weeping and rapture in one.[17]

Can we still dance like this today? The rabbi was burdened
with the sorrows and longings of his people. He wept. Yet
he danced. And the weeping and the rapture become one.
These men lived in such a way that the suffering of their
people were transformed for a few moments. Their down-
cast souls were recreated. They stood out from themselves
for a few hours. One Hasidic master spoke of the recreation
in the following words:

> The creation of heaven and of earth is the unfolding of some-
> thing out of nothing, the descent of the higher into the lower.
> But the holy men who detach themselves from being and ever
> cleave to God see and comprehend him in truth, as if there was
> now the nothing as before creation. They turn the something
> back into nothing. And this is the more wonderful: to raise
> up what is beneath. As it is written: "The last wonder is greater
> than the first."[18]

Such dancing does exist today not only in a Hasidic synagogue as I experienced a few years ago with Rabbi Shlomo
Carlbach, but also in the streets of Moscow. In 1965 and
1966 Elie Wiesel visited Moscow. He was drawn by the silent
cry of the Jews of this land. It was the evening of the feast of
Simchat Torah, the celebration of the completion of the
reading of the Torah. Jews—young and old, poor and rich,
educated and uneducated, believers and unbelievers, those
who are Jews only in name and birth and those who are

committed Jews—all these Jews, thousands of them (thirty or forty thousand by some counts) gathered outside the Central Synagogue. Many of these people were suffering from some kind of persecution. Their lives were steeped in fear. Yet they gathered publicly at the synagogue, "where they remained until almost dawn singing and dancing in Hasidic abandon."[19] For a few hours they were raised up and recreated. Their political situation did not change. But they were able to enter into it again with a bit more energy and courage. And by their wonder they continue to challenge our wonder.

The person caught in despair has little energy left for action. He or she feels that nothing really matters. For it is felt that nothing will really change. And yet, they realize that they have no choice but to continue on. To dance for a few moments, to long for a few moments, to wonder for a few moments does not change their condition in life. It merely lifts them They are quickened. "There are those who suffer very greatly and cannot tell what is in their hearts, and they go their ways full of suffering. But, if they meet someone whose face is bright with laughter, he can quicken them with his gladness. And it is no small thing to quicken a human being!"[20]

Finally, I would like to introduce you to a wonder-ful elderly lady. She is a fictional person. This lady, full of wonder, is a character in a novel and a film. Her name is Countess Mathilda Chardin but she is commonly known as Maude. Maude is a survivor of a Nazi concentration camp. Her interests ranged from funerals to a field of daisies, from births to motorcycles. Even though she was near her eightieth birthday, Maude was an explorer and always open to a new experience. Her wonder extended to anything and everything. She grew excited at a freshly baked cake as well

as at munching on a raw carrot. Everything and everyone
was precious for Maude, so precious that she was unpossessive: she could throw a gift in a lake and exclaim: "Now I'll
always know where it is."[21] Maude attempted to share her
spirit with a young man named Harold. That spirit is
summed up in her words to him when he found her crying.
She said:

> Yes. I cry. I cry for you. I cry for this [an old visa]. I cry at
> beauty—a sunset or a seagull. I cry when a man tortures his
> brother.... when he repents and begs forgiveness... when
> forgiveness is refused ... and when it is granted. One laughs.
> One cries. Two uniquely human traits. And the main thing in
> life, my dear Harold, is not to be afraid to be human.[22]

Maude is filled with wonder, a wonder that is at the source
of her smile as well as of her tears. She is a person whom
we know we cannot imitate. She is inimitable. Yet she
allows us to be free to smile and laugh and cry and, in all
this, to be wonderers. She can quicken another human
person. "And it is no small thing to quicken a human being."

This is the prayer of wonder—for some to be quickened
and for others to quicken. This is the marvel, the longing,
the expectation, the curiosity, the gentle questioning. It is
the coming alive for a few moments. And this itself is a
marvel, a wonder.

Notes

1. Antoine de Saint-Exupery, *The Little Prince* (New York:
Harcourt, Brace & World, 1943), p. 13.

2. Quoted in D. T. Suzuki, E. Fromm, R. DeMartino, *Zen Buddhism and Psychoanalysis* (New York: Grove, 1963), p. 1.
3. Lucien Stryk, Takoshi Ikemoto, ed. & trans., *Zen: Poems, Prayers, Sermons, Anecdotes, Interviews* (New York: Anchor, 1963), p. 17.
4. Luke 9:46.
5. Matthew 18:1–4.
6. Isaiah 65:19–24.
7. Revelation 21:3–4.
8. Daniel Berrigan as quoted by Robert Heyer, ed., *Discovery in Word* (New York: Paulist, 1968), p. 124.
9. Marilyn Harris, *Hatter Fox*, (New York: Bantam, 1974), p. 219.
10. Ibid., p. 219.
11. Mark 1:15.
12. Ephesians 3:14–19.
13. 1 Corinthians 2:9.
14. Cf. Matthew 13:44–46. It is interesting to note how the wonder can be taken from discovery by the law. A friend who is a law student mentioned to me that this particular parable of the treasure would be senseless in England because the man who found the treasure and spent his fortune would have wasted his worldly lot. Why? Treasure trove, by law belongs to the crown, not to its finder or the owner of the land where it is found. Hence, the law would dissipate the joy and wonder of discovery, unless, of course, the finder is the king or queen.
15. Cf. Cecile Bolling v. Goetz, "Christian mystic, scientist, priest," *The National Catholic Reporter* (February 17, 1965), p. 9.
16. Pierre Teilhard de Chardin, *The Divine Milieu* (New York: Harper and Row, 1960), p. 82.
17. Martin Buber, *The Legend of the Baal-Shem* (New York: Schocken, 1969), p. 21.
18. Ibid., p. 23.

19. Elie Wiesel, *Legends of Our Time* (New York: Avon, 1970), p. 184.
20. Martin Buber, *Ten Rungs: Hasidic Sayings* (New York: Schocken, 1962), pp. 44–45.
21. Colin Higgins, *Harold and Maude* (New York: Avon, 1975), p. 122.
22. Ibid., p. 126.

4

Prayer as Silence

Wonder can often give rise to silence, the wonderful gaze, the speechless tongue, the receptive heart-mind. To believe that life is mystery is to believe that beyond and in words there is silence. Mystery gives rise to wonder which precipitates silence which itself is the mystery. Moshe, the teacher of Elie Wiesel, had said that our questions would be answered by God but that we would not be able to understand the answer. To question is to take the risk of not understanding an answer if one comes. A further risk, however, is that of receiving no answer at all. No matter which predominates, there is silence.

Of the many kinds of silence there are two of which I will speak: an uneasy silence and a creative silence. Silence surrounds us. It can give rise to fear as in the tears of a young child left alone in a dark room at night. Or, it can caress you as the silence of the night while walking on a beach or through a forest. Or, it can create you as when the poet or painter rises to pen the words that have been yearning to be said or to paint that picture which has teased the imagination. Silence can be a bridge to others or it can divide a person from self and from others. It can be filled with joy and it can be filled with hurt and bitterness. Silence can be sterile or it can be creative. The second is what we seek, but how often we encounter the first!

43

I will speak first of the uneasy silence, which may, at times, have the seeds of creative silence within it.

At the beginning of a semester while many of my students are not totally familiar with my teaching style, some of these students experience an uneasy, anxious silence in class. Often after I ask a question of the class, a silence will take over the room. It is a time to think. The seconds pass slowly for some students. The silence becomes loud and anxious for them. For others, it is a quiet time to think. The uneasiness of the silence for some students is symptomatic of a difficulty some persons have with silence at any time. Something must be going on for these people at all times. They cannot stand the silence.

Another uneasy silence is heavy. A group of people sit together conversing quietly. Suddenly someone enters the room and announces that he has a message. The room becomes quiet with expectation. The man then communicates some bad news. His words are punctuated by silence. When he is finished, silence again takes over. The initial expectant silence has been transformed into an uneasy, sad silence.

Or, there is the silence of Hatter Fox, who while confined to her cell, refuses to speak with anyone. There is no one who has ever listened to her. She feels that no one will even hear her. Why, then, should she speak? Her silence is a challenge. It defies. And those who can hear this defiant silence, also become uneasy.

There is also an oppressive silence. Such silence was experienced by people who were escorted by a Nazi SS officer to barracks in a concentration camp where they were left standing, waiting. It is the silence of someone who is being treated unjustly.

And then there is a stoney silence.

In the Book of Ecclesiastes, Qoheleth proclaims: "Vanity of vanities. All is vanity! For all his toil under the sun, what does man gain by it?"[1] A person comes face to face with his or her own finiteness or impermanence and the perishableness of all that is done. There is nothing that has substance. All is empty. All is void. The silence that may engulf us when we come face to face with this condition may be creative, but it is more often uneasy. There is nothing to gain. All things pass. What is the use in even getting up in the morning. Nothing will grow in this desert where I am, in this desert who I am. Nothing can speak to my situation. The situation itself does not speak. This is a silence which is anxious, which leaves us helpless. Something of what I am trying to say is expressed in the following:

Hard turf silently softens under
    the gaze of a warm
        sun.
a debilitating lethargy seeps slowly
    into the bones—or out—
      so slowly and almost
      imperceptibly.
Both wanted and unwanted it is
    allowed to filter through
    the body to the
        mind.
There is nowhere to turn—it
    can't be stopped—
Familiar faces, longing eyes, encouraging,
voice, unspoken words, spanning hundreds
of miles—maybe a few feet,
the sound of a smooth guitar,
    a light voice,
      passion;
a paperback which once spoke so

eloquently—why not
now?
a God who is silent in the emptiness
of the phony—
nothing can satisfy,
nothing contain the flow,
no thing really matters—
what was alive in the morning is a
forgotten dream as the
body sags under the burden
of a bloodless heart.
everyone and no one is near,
as the unidentified self
reaches out and can't
say a word—for there is no word—
just blankness
that unsettles the stomach
in the face of a day
which has no promise,
a now which is dead and
a past which is a
dream.
you bite your finger or tongue;
but that is disappointing—no
thing, no one can
fill the gap,
so why . . .
(even that can be disconcerting)
. . . bother?
forget in the passage of a deep sleep?
it will return—it won't let go—
a few days or weeks, maybe—but
then. . .

These have been a few examples of experiences that
might give birth to an uneasy silence. There is another

uneasy silence which is more ambivalent. This silence is given expression by Isaiah when he says:

> The people that walked in darkness has seen a great light; on those who live in a land of deep shadow a light has shown.[2]

The silence is that of darkness, I might even say the dark night of the soul, a time of purgation, of purification. The storm is raging. A direction is seen. It is not yet taken. Is there the energy to go where I see I can go? Elie Wiesel suggests: "It is in the silence after the storm that God reveals himself to man. God is silence."[3] It is in this silence after the storm when we expect to be on the shore, but there is no land on the horizon. It is then that we can cry out with Isaiah: "Yahweh, can you go unmoved by all of this, oppressing us beyond measure by your silence?"[4] A response may return to us, again through Isaiah:

> From the beginning I have been silent, I have kept quiet, held myself in check. I groan like a woman in labor, I suffocate, I stifle.[5]

This is the God who spoke, and light was shed on the world. This is the God who creates, yet finds so many obstacles in the way of his creative power. "He" is long overdue. In "his" labor "he" is suffocating, stifled. Maybe this is what Dietrich Bonhoeffer meant when he wrote: "Man is challenged to participate in the sufferings of God at the hands of a godless world."[6] The godless person is the one who refuses to allow silence to speak creatively. To participate in the sufferings of God may be to continuously search for new ways to create in the midst of a suffocating, stifling cloud. It is being able to continue on, to rise out of bed in the morning and not know why or how it is done. Thomas Merton describes in detail the silence of which I am speaking, though he uses very different language. In his book *Contemplative Prayer,* while speaking of prayer in solitude he points out that the dimensions of this type of prayer "are those of man's ordinary anguish, his self-searching, his moments of nausea at his own vanity, falsity, and capacity for betrayal."[7] These are some of the elements of the ambiguity of which I spoke above: an exhilarating uneasiness and an agonizing creativity.

In order to be creative, the silence of prayer demands an intense listening by the one praying, not only to his or her own heart but also to the heart of the world. Merton develops this in regard to the prayer of the monk though he does not exclude the layperson who is also called to be a person of prayer. He writes:

> This is an age that, by its nature as a time of crisis, of revolution, of struggle, calls for the special searching and questioning which are the work of the monk in his meditation and prayer. For the monk searches not only his heart: he plunges deep into the heart of that world of which he remains a part although he seems to have "left" it. In reality the monk abandons the world only in order to listen more intently to the deepest and most neglected voices that proceed from its inner depth.[8]

In the silence which is darkness and exile and even despair, the worst is faced. In the silence, there can be listening. And out of that listening, a hearing. And from the hearing. . . .

There are other times, however, when silence means rest and quiet. The silent meditative prayer is not so much a way to the finding of God (which we still attempt) but rather a way of resting in the God who is near, whose presence is felt among us. This presence was described in the previous chapter on prayer as wonder. Wonder is a standing silent in the presence of the One who is to come and who is with us. This silence is not the silence of noiselessness nor is it the silence of boredom. It is rather the silence of "isness" which is "becoming."

Many object to this kind of silence. "It is a waste of time," they might say. Or, "What use does it have?" We are so used to having well-defined goals and putting our time to good use that we cannot forget about time. We get caught in time. But the silence of which I am now speaking is utterly useless. It does not have a goal. Hence, it cannot be exploited.

We attempt to gain status or success, power or pleasure, meaning or self-fulfillment. No one of these is the ultimate answer. At each point, we return to silence. Silence has nothing to gain nor to lose. We contemporary people do. We cannot stand being useless for very long. We must have a goal or purpose. But that very purpose or goal can give rise to anxiety and frustration and so often to exploitation insofar as one may step on another to reach that goal we set up for ourselves. But silence is useless. In this it is pure. It exists for nothing at all, yet by that very fact, encompasses all. It is the nothing created out of something.

So also prayer is useless. It serves no practical purpose, not even to relax the one praying. For once a person tries to relax, the very trying becomes an obstacle to the possibility of relaxing. Once, however, a person lets go, then the relaxation enters and the silence becomes pure, the silence enters with its creative power.

Finally, this silence does not only have to happen in a meditation hall or a chapel or even in one's room. It can happen there. But it can also happen when one is speaking or working or walking. For, in work which is really work and in speech which is really speech, that is, related work and related speech, silence is always present. In his novel, *Dawn*, Wiesel has one of his characters saying: "For half an hour, an hour, we walked in complete silence. At first I found the silence embarrassing, then to my surprise I began to enjoy it. The silence of two people is deeper than the silence of one. Involuntarily, I began to talk."[9] Silence is the context of the word and the deed. More than being their context, it is of their essence and substance. It is then a silence which thunders gently!

There are many other forms of creative silence. One is the thoughtful silence. A question is asked. The one questioned is not threatened but remains quiet for a few moments gathering thoughts and organizing them. Then out of this reflective, thoughtful silence, a response is made.

Silence may also be healing. Imagine a day during which demands are being made constantly. There is barely time to breathe. There is a longing for, at least, a few moments of quiet, of silence, time during which the person can gather their resources, regain strength. One Hasidic master would go so far as to say that unless a person has one hour a day to himself or herself, that person will not be human. Silence is not only the substance of the word and the deed. Silence is of the essence of being human.

I will conclude this chapter with three Hasidic anecdotes. I will comment on the first and then allow the next two to speak for themselves.

Rabbi Mendel once commented on the verse in the scriptures: "For God hath heard the voice of the lad." He explained it in this way: "Nothing in the preceding verses indicates that Ishmael cried out. No, it was a soundless cry, and God heard it."[10] What is a soundless cry? It is a silent cry. It is a cry from the heart that cannot or does not become a spoken word. Such a cry might express despair or hopelessness. But it also might be a person's only resistence to an uncontrollably painful existence. Nothing *said* would seem to be of help. Since such a cry comes from the heart, from a person's depth, it might be said that it is heard by God, the God who is the heart of our heart. But it might also be said that such a cry is heard by God since it is uttered by God in the heart of the person crying. It is heard by the God who is in sympathy with the one crying.

Rabbi Mendel's hasidim once sat at his table in silence. The silence was so profound that one could hear the fly on the wall. After grace, the rabbi of Biala said to his neighbor: "What a table we had today! I was probed so deeply that I thought my veins would burst, but I managed to hold out and answer every question I was asked."[11]

When Mendel was in Kotzk, the rabbi of that town asked him: "Where did you learn the art of silence?" He was on the verge of answering the question, but then he changed his mind and practiced his art.[12]

Notes

1. Ecclesiastes 1:2-3.
2. Isaiah 9:1.
3. Elie Wiesel, *The Gates of the Forest* (New York: Avon, 1967), p. 71.
4. Isaiah 64:11-12.
5. Isaiah 42:14.
6. Dietrich Bonhoeffer, *Letters and Papers from Prison* (New York: Macmillan, 1953), p. 222.

7. Thomas Merton, *Contemplative Prayer* (New York: Herder and Herder, 1969), p. 25.

8. Ibid., p. 25.

9. Elie Wiesel, *Dawn* (New York: Avon, 1970), p. 67.

10. Martin Buber, *Tales of the Hasidim: The Later Masters* (New York: Schocken, 1948), p. 301.

11. Ibid.

12. Ibid.

5

Prayer as Concentration

Raimundo Panikkar says that the essence of Hindu prayer could be summed up in one word—concentration. Often when Oriental prayer is discussed it is understood as a form of navel gazing or a looking at your nose or as a form of sophisticated introspection. Panikkar pointed out that this is precisely what it is not. He suggested that concentration is the finding of a center, the gathering around a point. It is the finding of the center of a sphere which is the whole of reality. In Christian terms, this might be described as the reconciliation of all things in Christ. It also may be spoken of in terms of recollection (a gathering together again) or meditation (finding a center, a midst, a middle).

It is very important that we understand from the beginning that the center is not our psychological ego. Prayer as concentration is not a sophisticated egoism. It is not even becoming aware of my self (ego), my private self, but rather, an awareness of living in a network of relations.

This last remark needs some clarification. We Westerners usually view the world and others as separate from ourselves. We are quite aware of individuality and uniqueness. What I wish to suggest here (and it will be developed more extensively in the following chapter) is that reality is not merely this, but that, at its root, reality is a network of relations. While each human person is unique, he or she is also related to all other persons and to the world. The primary fact is that of relation. "In the beginning is the relation," declares Martin Buber.[1] Thus, self is not defined in terms of a separate ego or as isolated from all else. Rather, self is understood in relation.

Meditation may begin with a looking into our own heart but it does not end there. For while looking at your own heart, if one concentrates, he or she can discover that it is the heart of the world. In other words, the network of relations is discovered.

One way of speaking of concentration is in terms of presence. If we think of ourselves as simply individuals, it is difficult, if not impossible, to see the interrelationships between individuals except in terms of a juxtaposition. For persons to be present to one another, for the world to be present to them and them to the world, there must exist an intrinsic relationship. We do not simply stand side by side, but there is an interpenetration of our very beings. The primary fact of existence is not "me" but rather "us" or "I in relation." To concentrate is to become this primary fact, to become present in the already existing fact of the relationship, that is, to realize our radical interconnection with others and the world.

In the biblical account of the meeting between Moses and his God at the burning bush, we hear Yahweh speaking of himself as "I am who am." This statement is quite individualistic. Another translation of this statement is "I will be for you as who I am shall I be for you." This latter translation contains the former but extends it and gives expression to a fundamental interrelationship between God and his people. God is for his people. He is related to them and hence present for them. This relationship is also expressed in the covenant. "I will be your God and you shall be my people." God and his people are present to each other. The center is designated. It is both God and his people.

There are certain characteristics of prayer as concentration which also point to the meaning of presence. Often concentration and presence are conceived of as states of inertia, or unawareness. The opposite, however, is true. Concentration, as the gathering of energies, heightens awareness. It is the condition pointed to by Paul when he says: "Wake up from your sleep, rise from the dead."² The awareness of which I speak here is not an overawareness, that is, an awareness centered on one's ego. Rather it is an awareness of what I am doing but not in such a way that the awareness gets in the way of the action. This awareness is being present.

The presence of which I am speaking can also be discussed in terms of a sense of proportion. This sense of proportion is exhibited by God in the story of Jonah. In the story of Jonah, most of us remember that he was swallowed by a whale. Very few recall the conclusion. Jonah had been sent to the city of Nineveh to call the people there to repentance. A time limit was set when this great city would be destroyed. But the people repented and the disaster was averted. Jonah was very upset by this. He wanted God to destroy the city as was promised. Thus, Jonah left the city and sought shade from the burning sun. God saw to it that a casteroil plant should grow up over Jonah to give him shade. Jonah was delighted with the plant. The next day, God arranged that a worm should attack the plant, which it did, and the plant withered. Jonah was upset, even to the point of death. Yahweh said to him: "You are only upset about a casteroil plant which

cost you no labor. . . . Am I not to feel sorry for Nineveh?"
Jonah had lost all sense of proportion. He had become
overly upset about a plant. God had been upset with the
people of Nineveh, but when they repented he did not go
ahead with his plans to destroy the city. He was not overly
upset but had retained a sense of proportion.

A sense of proportion is also very much like the middle
way of the Buddha. The phrase "middle way" is often
interpreted as the avoidance of extremes in living, the
finding of a balance. If a person tries to find a balance, as
difficult as this is, that person will always end up with some
imbalance or with total inactivity. The middle way, however, is a relationship to life such that life does not present
itself as a choice between extremes. A person who is concentrated, who is present, can act with a sense of proportion, without getting overly upset.

A sense of proportion might be misunderstood to be a
balance. Not getting overly upset might also be seen as
having the same attitude—calm—in every situation. However, this is not what I mean by a sense of proportion. It is
not a balance. Rather, I mean that one responds to what is
demanded by the situation. There is no one way to respond which might be called proportionate. Rather, the
proportion is discovered in each unique situation. The response of a person in different situations may exhibit different degrees of "upsetness," more or less in accord with
the demands. Thus, "not to get overly upset" does not
mean the same attitude for all situations, but rather, "not
getting overly upset" in this particular situation. Thus, I
can be very upset but not necessarily overly upset in respect to one or another situation. The point is not so much
the degree of upsetness, but rather a presence in the situation, and a response to what the situation calls for.

Another aspect of prayer as concentration which involves presence is a sense of proportion in regard to time and space. Often the past or the future might take over our lives. We might try to live in the past, or we might try to live only for the future. In both cases, the present is ignored. A sense of proportion in regard to time is not to overemphasize either the past or the future but to allow the past and the future to speak to us what they have to say in the present. To be present is to live in the present. To live in the present is not a denial of the past and future but rather the integration of them. Living in the present, the fulltime present, affirms the past as leading to itself and the future as leading from itself. But such fulltime living is not only linear, as just described. The present is also filled with both past and future, both of which make the present to be what it is. It is generally clear to us how the past can be carried into the present. For example, memory involves the making present of the past. Also, from another angle, my past is part of what I am today. However, it is often not as clear how the future impinges on the present. One might think: "The future has not happened yet. How can it be present?" Yet a person often does project himself or herself into the future by plans made or goals or expectations. These projections enter into the present and affect the way of being present. Even if the ends have been unrealized, they have entered our present and shaped it to some extent. In other words, the future is projected into the present. Hence, fulltime present is a present that is constituted by past and future not merely in a linear fashion but in a simultaneous fashion. Thus, one can live in the past and for the future simultaneously. To do this is to live in the present. A sense of proportion in regard to time is to allow the past to be what it is in the present and to allow the future to be what it is in the present and to allow the two to enter into a dialogue in the meeting of what is happening.

A sense of proportion with respect to space can be seen in terms of place. There are many times when one might wish to be somewhere other than where he or she is at the moment. There might be a good reason for this longing. Often nothing can really be done to alter the circumstances. We can become overly upset and the situation can become worse. A sense of proportion here would be neither to get out nor to give in. Nor is a sense of proportion a sense of endurance. An Hasidic master once commented that the real exile of Israel in Egypt was that they began to endure it.

To be present is to be where we are when we are there, to do what we are doing when we are doing it. Soon after the death of Rabbi Moshe, Rabbi Mendel of Kotzk asked one of his disciples: "What was most important to your teacher?" The disciple replied: "Whatever he happened to be doing at the moment." To be present where one is, to do what one is doing is to be related to it and to allow it to be related to you. This is not simply doing one thing at the time or place. It might mean being present to the many things that are being demanded at this particular moment. Often concentration is incorrectly interpreted as doing one thing at a time. This interpretation, it seems to me, leaves too many people out, for example parents or teachers who are called upon to respond to many calls at the same time. Concentration also means to be responsive to many simultaneous demands, deciding which one to respond to initially, establishing a hierarchy of values such that each demand be met, or only one or even none depending on the demands and the resources one has to meet those demands. To be present in terms of doing what one is doing is to find the relationship which exists at the moment and to express that relationship in the action. The moment here is a fulltime moment which contains the past, the present, and the future.

Flowing directly from concentration, presence, and a sense of life as a network of relation is a deep compassion for all living creatures. Compassion is an essential element of prayer, no matter what religious tradition is being expounded. In the Jewish scriptures, for example, one way by which it is given expression is in terms of love of the stranger:

> It is he who sees justice done for the orphan and the widow, who loves the stranger and gives him food and clothing. Love the stranger, then, for you were strangers in the land of Egypt.[3]

Such love is not a patronizing love but a love which derives from a communion between the people involved. It arises out of a sense of relation in the network of relations.

This spirit of compassion is also given expression in the famous Hindu classic, the *Bhagavad Gita*. While speaking of the true yogi who sees God in all things and all things in God and who is in union with that God, the author adds:

> Who burns with the bliss
> And suffers the sorrow
> Of every creature
> Within his own heart,
> Making his own
> Each bliss and each sorrow
> Him I hold the highest
> Of all the yogis.[4]

The true yogi is not simply isolated from others in meditative splendor. Rather, the true yogi can feel and think and be identified with any other in joy or in sorrow, in pain or in bliss. The true yogi not only realizes that he or she is related to other persons insofar as we all belong to the same species. The yogi also realizes that each of us is intrinsically related in a network of relations and that each joy and sorrow is his or her own.

The same is true of the committed disciple of Jesus. Compassionate identification is at the heart of Jesus' eschatological discourse: "I tell you most solemnly, insofar as you did this to one of the least of these brothers of mine, you did it to me."[5]

Compassionate identification is also embedded in the spirit of Hasidism. The Baal Shem once exclaimed: "To pull another out of the mud, man must step into the mud himself."[6] Such a spirit is further expressed in a story from the tradition of Rabbi Nahman of Bratzlav. I will paraphrase the story. In a far country, there lived a prince who lost his mind and thought that he was a dog. All day, he walked on all fours and would accept only scraps to eat. His father, the king, was desperate and sent for anyone—from medical specialists to miracle workers—to cure his son. All failed. Then an unknown sage came and said he thought he could cure the prince. The king allowed him to try. Immediately, the sage removed his clothes and joined the prince on the floor, barking and playing. Initially, the prince was upset and apprehensive, but gradually he accepted the sage-dog and the two became fast friends. Then the sage put on a shirt. The prince was unbelieving: "Why should a dog wear a shirt?" The sage responded: "We all know that a dog is a dog no matter what is being worn." The same conversation took place when the sage began to eat like humans and then to act entirely like humans. The prince followed and was convinced and resumed his life as a prince.[7]

To pray is to concentrate, which is to be present. To be present is to enter upon a work or a conversation or leisure without any obstacles. It is to meet the other as other and yet to be related to that person. It is to be able to make present as many of one's resources as are available at this time and place, no matter how great or small these resources may be. Even if there are no resources, this also can be made available. For example, if you are asked to do something by another or asked to listen to another and know that at the time you are unable to respond, then this fact can be communicated to the person who is asking.

Prayer as concentration involves the focusing of one's self, the gathering together of energy, the being whole or integral which is holiness. Thus, it is not as important to say prayers as it is to be the prayer, to be whole, to be holy. The wholeness of which I speak is not an ideal unity, but rather a wholeness of response in the present, a wholeness of response in proportion to one's resources in the present.

Prayer as concentration is not an escape from the world nor is it a substitute for action. One can act when action is called for and be still when quiet is demanded. This is the everactive, everquiet spirit spoken of by Augustine of Hippo.

Prayer as concentration is not only a listening to the event or to the person, but a realization of the communion that is the basic condition of each person with the world and with other persons. It is having one's roots dug into the heart of the world, the Silence, which extends into our own hearts. This kind of prayer has no limits. It cannot be defined. Its only limits are those of authentic human existence itself. And that limit is Mystery.

Notes

1. Martin Buber, *I and Thou,* trans. W. Kaufmann (New York: Scribner, 1970), p. 69.
2. Ephesians 5:14.
3. Deuteronomy 10:18-19.
4. *Bhagavad Gita,* trans. Swami Prabhavananda and Christopher Isherwood (New York: Mentor, 1944), p. 67.
5. Matthew 25:40.
6. Elie Wiesel, *Souls on Fire* (New York: Random House, 1972), p. 20.
7. Ibid., pp. 170-171.

6

Prayer as Relatedness

Herman Melville wrote somewhere that "our lives are connected by a thousand threads." In the previous chapter, I referred to prayer as concentration in the context of reality understood as a network of relations. To concentrate is to gather one's energies or to find a center that is not so much our individual ego as a center in a network of relations. In the chapters on prayer as questioning, wonder, and silence, the working assumption was reality as a network of relations. To question is to ask about that network, to seek out the connections and spaces in it. To wonder involves a curiosity about the network and a marveling and fascination with it. To be silent is a condition in which the connections or spaces may be either difficult to discern or, on the contrary, quietly realized and forged, or felt to be ambiguous. Each of these experiences was seen to be prayer. Insofar as they are rooted in relatedness, then, the experience of relatedness is prayer. It is the purpose of this chapter[1] to present a broad, panoramic view of reality as a network of relations, in its structure and its dynamics. The structure of the network, I would suggest, is the basic context of prayer. The dynamics of the network are the activities of prayer. Prayer is both the realization and actualization of the network, the being and doing of the network.

The network of relations in which we are involved is quite complex. It may be broadly described, using a word coined by Raimundo Panikkar, as "cosmotheandric."[2] This word attempts to join together three dimensions of reality that are often perceived today as separate: the world or the cosmos, the human, and the divine. Relatedness happens within each of these three dimensions of reality as well as among them. Thus in the cosmic dimension, relatedness involves nature. In the human dimension relatedness involves the self and its relation with other selves. In the divine dimension, relatedness involves God's inner life. However, relatedness does not stop within the three dimensions. It is fundamental to the interplay of the three dimensions. The world, the human, and the divine dimensions of reality are inextricably related with each other. Thus relatedness within self, nature, and God as well as among self, nature, and God is the realization of a cosmotheandric network of relations. The life of each human person is a life in which some of these relations are recognized, some are recognized and realized, still others neither recognized nor realized and others are strained. Life, in fact, can be seen as the continuous recognition and realization of the complex network of relations in which we live and move and are. It is my contention that the living of this life is to pray.

Relatedness is often understood to be a condition in which disunity and disharmony are replaced by unity or harmony. The unity of the cosmotheandric network, however, is a unity that involves diversity as necessary for itself. The network cannot be reduced to a basic unity nor to a mere juxtaposition of its major elements. Rather this network is a unity in diversity and a diversity in unity.

One essential "object" (or should I say "subject"?) of relatedness is the "self." During a typical day I might experience not myself but rather myselves or the many different selves who I am. These many selves may be seen as "roles" that I would choose to play or into which I have flowed. Thus I might experience myself as a teacher or as a friend or as a priest, or therapist, or student, or antagonist. Furthermore, in each of these "roles" I might experience myself in many different ways. I am not exactly the same self for each of my friends or for each of my students, and so on. It might seem that, with so many roles and so many ways of being in each role, I would become confused. But this is not the case. Nor is it the case for very many people. Even though each of us is manifest in many different ways, we do not feel fragmented because of that. We do not suffer, except rarely, the deep pain of one of my former students who confided to me that she could not be with more than one friend at the same time. She felt very comfortable with each friend when they were alone together. But when she was in the presence of two or more of her friends she did not know who to be. Her question was: what person should I be when I am with this person or with that person? This young woman felt the deep pain of fragmentation. Her many selves were separate. Most of us are, more or less, all of a piece, though each of us will suffer some form of fragmentation at some time or in some relationship. We human persons experience ourselves as a self and as selves. We are all of a piece—one self and many selves.

Being all of a piece is the dynamic condition that the psychologist Carl Rogers describes as being congruent. Most of us rarely use the word congruent in relation to ourselves. This word usually conjures up memories of high school geometry where we encountered congruent triangles or rectangles or some other congruent figures. One triangle is congruent to another triangle if they fit exactly together. This geometric meaning is close to the meaning of Rogers who suggests that he experiences congruence in himself when, at some particular moment, what he is experiencing is present in his awareness and in his communication. Thus his experience and awareness and communication fit together, or are all of a piece. There is a unity of the diverse elements of experience, awareness, and communication. It is during these moments that Rogers feels himself to be congruent or "real."

I would also suggest that the persons described above as being both one self and many selves can be congruent. These persons have discovered a "fit." Their many selves are not merely separate but also "fit" together in some way. It may not be the same "fit" all the time. In fact, it rarely may be exactly the same "fit." Nor is there some ideal "fit" or mold that a person should squeeze into. Rather, a person is involved in a process of self-relatedness, a process that is ongoing and dynamic, always seeking and trying and changing within different situations, yet simultaneously stable and confident.

Such stability and confidence, however, is not always our experience. Often, I might be unaware of my experience, of what I think or feel or do. At another time or place, I might be aware of my experience but do not or am not able to communicate it. At such times, I experience incongruence. I am not totally related with myself. Another experience of incongruence is the experience of the young women described above. Her experience included an overawareness of one particular self to the exclusion of other selves. Such an experience might be described as a fixation in one of the many selves who I am. A fixation may appear as congruence or integration and there are times when it might be quite comfortable. But it also might be a repression of all but one of our many possible selves. When this is the case, such a person, sadly, cannot experience himself or herself in a dynamic manner, but is caught. Most tragic in this state of being is that the person is often unaware of her or his fixation even though they may be aware of some unidentified uneasiness. Thus the experience of incongruency can be found at two levels: the inability to relate our many selves and/or the unawareness of the unrelated condition.

I will conclude this discussion of relatedness with self by sharing an Hasidic tale that touches me deeply in its challenge. A Hasid in Eastern Europe committed himself to fast from food and drink from one Sabbath to the next. On the Friday afternoon at the end of the week, the Hasid became thirsty. He saw some water, went to it, and readied himself to drink. But instantly he realized that he would be breaking his commitment and that it was close to the end of the weeklong fast. He did not drink. But a few moments later he felt proud that he had overcome the temptation. On becoming aware of this pride, he argued with himself that it would be better to drink the water, break the commitment to fast rather than to fall prey to pride. The man then returned to the water and was ready to drink it when he noticed that he was no longer thirsty. In a while the Sabbath began and the Hasid entered the house of his teacher. As he crossed the threshold, the teacher said to him: "Patchwork."[3] According to Martin Buber, who wondered why this man, who had overcome his temptation not only to break his fast but also to pride, was treated so harshly, the object of the teacher's reproof is the wavering quality of the man's action. The work was not all of a piece. It was not done entirely from a related heart.

The object of formal meditation has often been presented to be the enterprise of discovering the heart of oneself, the discovery of an integration of the many selves who are in the heart that is the center of these selves. Such a process, however, is not characteristic only of formal meditation. It is built into the life process of each person. Formal meditation may be a great aid to this human process. But the process itself is meditative or prayerful even when not recognized in a formal manner.

Self-relatedness is only one aspect of the work in which we are involved, the task of recognizing and actualizing the complex of relations in our network of relations. Another aspect of human relatedness is with respect to other human persons.

There are numerous books and articles and workshops, both popular and professional, that are concerned with the development of interpersonal relations. Such a concern is central to relatedness with others which involves not only the repair of a broken relationship but also the realization of relationships in the network that had never been recognized. My concern here will be only with a few of the elements of this complex network of interpersonal relationships.

In general, relatedness with others involves not only the finding of connections with other people but also finding the spaces between oneself and another person(s). A Chinese Taoist story of a butcher who never sharpened his knives begins to illustrate the significance of spaces in the network of relations. After butchering for more than fifty years without sharpening his knives the butcher was asked why he didn't need to sharpen them. He responded by describing the meat as both solid and as containing interstices or spaces and then by pointing out that when he cut the meat, he did so by passing the knife through the interstices. Hence there was no resistance, no obstacle for the knife to overcome and the knives remained sharp.[4] The butcher was skilled enough to find the spaces. The same is true in the actualization of the interpersonal relations embedded in the basic network of relations.

Another story, from the Hasidic tradition, points in the same direction:

> Rabbi Abraham was asked: "Our sages say: 'And there is not a thing that has not its place.' And so man too has his own place. Then why do people sometimes feel so crowded?" He replied: "Because each wants to occupy the place of another."[5]

To be related with another means, among other things, that we give the other space to be a unique person by neither trying to control that other nor by being a parasite on that other person. It is to allow the other to occupy his or her own place. Karl Rahner suggests something similar in reference to unity in the church. He says that the only thing that will bring unity on the human level is to love another enough to allow that other to be different.[6] I would add that the difference is not only that between persons but also the difference a person may be from himself or herself. Another Hasidic story illustrates this point. The story refers to God, but I believe it also is significant for interpersonal relations:

> A disciple asked the Baal-Shem: "Why is it that one who clings to God and knows he is close to him, sometimes experiences a sense of interruption and remoteness?" The Baal-Shem explained: "When a father sets out to teach his little son to walk, he stands in front of him and holds his two hands on either side of the child, so that he cannot fall, and the boy goes toward his father between his father's hands. But the moment he is close to his father, the father, moves away a little, and

holds his hands farther apart, and he does this over and over, so that the child may learn to walk.[7]

With a few changes in appropriate places, this story could also be about a deep friendship in which the persons involved not only recognize the connections and affinity between themselves but also are conscious of the uniqueness of each other and the necessity of the other to be truly other in order for the relationship to be truly mutual.

Up to this point I have pointed out the creative dimension of the spaces between people. There are moments, however, when a relationship becomes strained. The lines of connection in the network become tight and tense. The space, now, does not enoble the connection but rather manifests an unease or anxiety or anger or disturbance of the relation. What must be done? What can be done? One possibility is to pull away from the relation, to imagine that it does not exist. Sometimes, sadly, this is all that can be done for the sake of the personal sanity of the people involved. Then it would be better, it seems, not to repress the relationship but to face the fact that it cannot develop further, that the distance between the persons is too great and too treacherous for either to navigate. One hope, however, does exist. It is found in the possibility of the people involved trying to keep an eye open for possible bridges that might arise accidentally (the people involved may feel too hurt and too vulnerable to have the energy to take the risky first step). A second possibility is to give in. While this might release the strain for the persons involved, it would also mean that one person is now under the control of the other. Hence, while one strain is relaxed, another begins to develop. A third possibility that I see is that at least one of the persons continuously seeks to ease the strain by risking communication in which the strain is clarified for both persons who then seek a way to ease it. A few other ways by which relatedness with others is blocked are stereotyping and the use of defense mechanisms. To stereotype another person is to totally define that person on a general basis in terms of, for example, their background, religion, race, or another category. Stereotyping blocks relatedness by destroying the uniqueness of a person. I can never be related with a person if I simply see them to be merely a general type rather than as a particular person.

Another obstacle is a defense mechanism. Psychologists have suggested often that these measures are not only protective of the self but also destructive of an honest relation. I will mention briefly four such mechanisms that are widely used. In general, a person is usually not conscious that he or she is engaged in using a defense mechanism. The four I will touch upon are: rationalization, projection, reaction formation, and repression.

Rationalization involves giving a good reason for what I do even if it is not the real reason.

Projection is a protective measure by which I do not recognize some of my own bad qualities and then I attribute such qualities in some exaggerated form to other people.

In reaction formation, a person tries to hide a motive or feeling or value by expressing, in very strong terms, the opposite motive or feeling or value.

Finally, a repression is the public denial of a personal impulse or tendency or wish that the person desires to keep in check.

In the past few pages, I have touched on some creative and destructive spaces between people. Relatedness with others, as an aspect of our cosmotheandric network, also involves an awareness and actualization of the interconnections among people. This task is initiated by a person who takes a risk by addressing or responding to another with courage. When a connection is realized, it is characterized by many qualities described in previous chapters, especially trust, wonder, and presence. Interconnectedness also involves mutuality, directness, sharing, caring, respecting, knowing the other, and responsibility.

In short, relatedness with an other, given an absence of destructive spaces or connections, encompasses the continual development of the connections and spaces between the persons.

I will conclude this section with two quotes, one from Elie Wiesel and the other from Carl Rogers. Wiesel describes how a bridge can be built between persons when he writes:

> We are alone, but we are capable of communicating to one another both our loneliness and our desire to break through it. You say, "I'm alone." Someone answers, "I'm alone too." There's a shift in the scale of power. A bridge is thrown between the two abysses.[8]

On the other hand, Carl Rogers, comparing people to sunsets, affirms their uniqueness and his unwillingness to control their beauty:

> People are just as wonderful as sunsets, if I can let them be. In fact, perhaps the reason we can truly appreciate a sunset is that we cannot control it. When I look at a sunset as I did the other evening I don't find myself saying, "soften the orange a little on the right hand corner, and put more purple along the base, and use a little more pink in the cloud color." I don't do that. I don't try to control a sunset. I watch it with awe as it unfolds.[9]

Each unique person is as wonderful as a sunset. No person should be controlled but allowed to unfold. Yet, at the same time, in our network of relations, people are connected, and it must be recognized by everyone that either the activity or inactivity of each one affects the others. What is unfolding is not simply the individual person but also the network of relations itself. Prayer as relatedness involves the realization and actualization of the network of relations in oneself and with others.

A second major element of the cosmotheandric network for which relatedness is not only of utmost necessity but is axiomatic, is nature. In the previous pages, the human element of the network was discussed. At this point the relation between the human and the cosmic or worldly elements will be briefly pointed to.

Insofar as reality is a network of relations, those relations are not simply among humans but also between humans and the rest of the natural universe. Appearances suggest our separateness and these appearances do not lie. But they also do not tell the whole truth. Not only am I, as a human being, born *into* the world, I am also born *out of* or *from* the world. My connection with the so-called outside world is an intrinsic connection. I breathe and the line of my breath is a lifeline within the cosmotheandric network of relations.

The ecological network is clearly expressed in a story and its commentary. It seems that an aquarium ran short of sea water just as it received a shipment of live salt water creatures. The curators of the aquarium, since the formula for sea water is known, decided to manufacture some salt water. When this task was completed, they put the creatures into the aquarium newly filled with the manufactured sea water. The creatures soon died. Then some real sea water was added to the manufactured water, some creatures put into it, and these creatures lived. The implications of this experiment are that not only do the many drops of water in the great oceans comprise a life of their own but also that this life in the drop of water makes possible the life of the creatures that live within it. But this is not all. Our own human life is also dependent on the life of the oceans. Our life is linked in a basic way with that of the ocean. If the oceans died, the death knell for humans and all other creatures would not be far behind. Some effects of ocean death would be a rise in temperature and the melting of the icecaps at the North and South Poles, causing floods. Then there would be rainlessness and hence global drought and famine. A final effect would be loss of the oxygen supply. I have drawn out this description to illustrate the intimate connection between the human and the cosmic and to point out that relatedness with nature is as important as relatedness with ourselves and with other humans.

In the gospel according to Matthew we read that we humans are the salt of the earth. This comment points to our relation with the cosmos. Salt is a condiment that draws out the flavor of the food on which it is used. Humans can draw the flavor out of the earth. By reason of human consciousness, the cosmos would seem to become conscious of itself. However, we must also realize that the earth is the necessary ground of our life. Prayer as relatedness does not only involve ourselves and others. It is also an ecological enterprise. Insofar as we humans have some power to manipulate the lands and the seas, we must also be aware of the intrinsic network of relations that exists among the various natural elements as well as be-

tween ourselves and nature. Prayer as relatedness includes
nature. It is wonderful and awesome. Yet, hopefully, it will
arise out of and lead to a relation that transcends manipu-
lation. These are some of the implications of the meditative walk in the woods or contemplative sojourn by the sea.

A third element of the cosmotheandric network is the
divine. This element is both the root and the term of the
other elements. It is their context and their horizon. They
do not exist without it. Nor does the divine exist without
the human and the cosmic.

What is the significance of the divine dimension? Each
human person can experience the unmeasurable depth of
his or her being. Each person can also experience the inexhaustible complexity of the network of relations in
which we live. That network is not experienced simply as a
premade, unchangeable network but as everchanging and
everchangeable. No person, no element of the network, no
dimension of the network is a merely closed being. Living
in the network we are continuously touched by other elements. We are more than the particular and private aspects of our lives. There is always more than meets the eye
or touches the heart. It is this "evermore" character of life in
the network that I would like to refer to as the divine
dimension of the cosmotheandric network of relations.

This depth dimension is present in both the human and
the cosmic dimensions. And it is also present in the relations among these dimensions. The divine dimension,
however, is not the center of the network. In a very real
sense, each point of the network (involving all three dimensions: cosmic, human, and divine) can be conceived of
as a center. God is, as it were, in need of the cosmic and the
human as they are in need of God.

Usually, when one is speaking of prayer, it is relatedness

with God that is emphasized. Yet if I only focus here I might miss the entire network. In fact, I would suggest that one will miss the divine dimension if one merely focuses on it. Then the focus would eliminate the other dimensions within which the divine is recognized. To pursue the depth of my relation with myself, with other people, and with the cosmos is to pursue the depth of reality which is God. To stop short of this depth is to stop short of relatedness within the cosmotheandric network, to ignore a central dimension of reality, the "evermore" of the dynamic exchange among the various dimensions in which we live and change and die.

In conclusion, I would like to share the power of the story of the Little Prince as manifesting the power of relatedness. The Prince had become a close friend of a fox. Once the two had become intimate, they had to separate. The fox shared a secret with the Prince. He said to him: "It is only with the heart that one can see rightly: what is essential is invisible to the eye."[10] To see rightly, I would suggest, is to see relatedly, to see in the context of the ties that are a part of our life in the network and to see in the light of the spaces between the elements of the network. This is illustrated by a conversation between the Little Prince and the fox about "taming." What does it mean—to tame? And the fox said, while pointing out that it is an act too often neglected, that taming means to establish ties. And while their ties were being established the Prince and the fox became increasingly aware of their uniqueness, of the creative spaces between them.[11] To be related in a continuous life process is to realize and to establish or constitute the ties or relations and the spaces in which each of us is involved. Unless prayer happens in this context, it remains without its heart. But not only is the cosmotheandric network the context of prayer. Prayer is the vibrant dynamism of the network itself.

Notes

1. I have placed this chapter here rather than at the beginning of the book, because I preferred to share with the reader more familiar aspects of the human roots of prayer before presenting the less familiar vision of reality suggested in the present chapter.
2. I am deeply indebted to Raimundo Panikkar for his fundamental cosmotheandric intuition. This intuition is extensively described in his essay, "Colligite Frgmenta: For an Integration of Reality," which may be found in *From Alienation to Atoneness* edited by Francis A. Eigo (Villanova: Villanova University Press, 1977), pp. 19ff. In 1974, I had heard Panikkar deliver an address that was the basis for this essay. This address helped me to begin to integrate many insights that I had gathered through reading and conversation.
3. Martin Buber, *Hasidism and Modern Man* (New York: Harper Torchbook, 1966), pp. 146–147.
4. I do not know the exact source of this story. It was told to me about ten years ago by my teacher, Bernard Phillips.
5. Martin Buber, *Tales of the Hasidim: The Later Masters* (New York: Schocken, 1948), p. 72.
6. Cf. Karl Rahner, *The Dynamic Element in the Church* (New York: Herder and Herder, 1964), p. 74.
7. Martin Buber, *Tales of the Hasidim: The Early Masters* (New York: Schocken, 1947), p. 65.

8. Elie Wiesel, *The Gates of the Forest* (New York: Avon, 1967), p. 178.
9. Carl Rogers, "Some Elements of Effective Interperson Communication." The source of this article is unknown to me. The content of it, however, is very much in accord with Roger's other writings.
10. Antoine de Saint-Exupery, *The Little Prince* (New York: Harcourt, Brace & World, 1943), p. 70.
11. Ibid., pp. 65–66.

7

Prayer as Perceptiveness

A prayerful person is a person who is rooted in the cosmotheandric network of relations. Prayer involves both the realization and actualization of that network in the forms of questioning, wonder, silence, and concentration. Each of these human experiences is grounded, to some degree, in the human ability to perceive. Thus a perceptive person is a prayerful person. The traditional forms of meditation and contemplation profoundly affect a person's perception of reality. It is not the purpose of this chapter to discuss exhaustively and scientifically the physiological and psychological and sociological investigations of perception. I will, rather, draw the broad lines of what it means to be a perceptive person. By doing this, I suggest that the development of perceptiveness by a person is also the development of prayerfulness.

Who, then, is a perceptive person? The response to this question will enable us to uncover how perceptiveness is prayerfulness. In general, a perceptive person is a person who is "in touch with" himself or herself, and with the cosmos and with God, that is, a person who is "in contact with" the cosmotheandric network in which we live and of which we are a fundamental dimension. The image of "touch" is very powerful and sensuous. It is used here, initially, to refer to all our senses: sight, hearing, tasting, smelling, and, of course, touching. Hence, it is sensuous. "Touch" is powerful insofar as it points to a double movement of each human person and hence to a dual operation in perceptivity. This dual operation involves both a "taking in" of impressions and also a "giving out" of expressions. "Touch," then, is impressive. When a person is "in touch" that person feels or "takes in" something. "Touch" is also expressive. It is a person's moving beyond himself or herself to share with another. Perceptiveness, as being "in touch" is, then, an operation by which life flows through our fundamental network of relations. To be a perceptive person, in the sense outlined above, is to be alive, to be impressive (to take in) and to be expressive (to put out).

A common understanding of perceptiveness focuses on its receptive character. This insight is expressed in the many words used to describe a perceptive person. Such a person is observant, open, tuned in, a good listener. The perceptive person recognizes or "picks up" the feelings of others, notices small changes, has all his or her antennae out. Not only does this person "pick up" or "take in" sense impressions but also the moods or the feelings that these impressions suggest. Thus the perceptive person is "in touch" with the heart of the other, is not only sympathetic but also empathetic. The other refers to both other people and nature. A perceptive person is able to listen to and to hear another and to "take in" that other. However, the process of "taking in" is not symbiotic. The other is allowed to be other. The spaces are recognized and respected. A perceptive person imagines the other not on his or her own terms or as a projection of self, but rather on the ground of the other. The perceptive person is in touch with self but not centered on self. This person is able to go beyond self toward the other, to receive the other and yet allow the other to remain other while also remaining one-self. The receptivity involved in perceptiveness includes both identification and separation. A few stories will illustrate some of the dynamics just described. A university professor once inquired about Zen. He was received by a Zen Master who immediately served tea. The master poured the professor's cup full and then kept on pouring. The professor watched this and then exclaimed: "Stop! It's already full. No more will go in." The master replied: "You are like this cup, full of your own ideas and opinions. How can I show you Zen unless you first empty your cup?"[1] The perceptive person is one with an empty cup and hence is a person who is able to receive with freshness and newness. One effect of Zen meditation is the emptying of the cup, the change of perception by which a person's own concepts and ideas do not get into the way of their relation with another.

In an Hasidic story we are told that the great Maggid of Mezritch once said to his disciples: "I shall teach you the best way to say Torah. You must cease to be aware of yourselves. You must be nothing but an ear which hears what the universe of the word is constantly saying within you. The moment you start hearing what you yourself are saying, you must stop."[2] A perceptive person listens to the other as the Hasidic disciple is called upon to listen to Torah.

Another story. The delightful Sufi, Nasrudin, went to see a rich man and asked: "Give me some money." The rich man replied, "Why?" Nasrudin said: "I want to buy an elephant," to which the rich man said, "If you have no money, you can't afford to keep an elephant." "I came here," said Nasrudin, "to get money, not advice."[3] A perceptive person, unlike the rich man, listens to and hears only what is said. A person can become perceptive by emptying their cup, listening to the other and hearing only what is said.

However, if we stop here, we will receive only a partial understanding of perceptiveness, its receptive dimension, its impressiveness. A perceptive person is also expressive. Our senses are not only receptors of impressions but also the very ways by which we give or "put out" expressions. There are two different ways of expression inherent in perceptiveness: a perceptive person not only hears the other but also responds to the other; and, a perceptive person manifests who he or she is in the process of perceptiveness.

A perceptive person not only notices or observes the moods or feelings or changes in others but also gives expression to what is noticed. The expression may be verbal or nonverbal. Such an expression is a response which may simply reflect what is perceived by the observer. It is always, however, a response to what is "seen." For example, one person might perceive that another person is overjoyed, knows this, and manifests it. The observer can then respond to what is seen, the consciously manifest joy of another. On another occasion a person might notice that a friend is overwrought about a separation yet not able to deal with the feelings the separation involves. Here the response is more complex than the one to the overjoyed person. Here the response would have to consider not only the painful feeling of separation but also the inability to face these feelings. My fundamental point here is simply that perceptiveness is manifest in both receptivity *and* response.

A second way by which expression is inherent in perceptiveness is partially described by Bernard Lonergan when he writes:

> Our perceiving is not just a function of the impressions made on our senses. It has an orientation of its own and it selects, out of a myriad of others, just those impressions that can be constructed into a pattern with meaning.[4]

What I select to "see" says something about who I am. Perceptiveness is not simply passive. It is also active. A person perceives according to who he or she is. Perceptiveness is expressive of this identity of a person. Our flesh and bones, our bodies are powerful symbols. Our senses are part of this bodily symbol. A person who "looks" not only "takes in" what is seen, but also manifests something about himself or herself in the way of looking, for example, intense, relaxed, anxious, perturbed; and also in what is selected to be received.

In summary, perceptiveness is a cybernetic process involving both a "taking in" and a "putting out," receiving and responding, impressing and expressing. Unless both of these elements are operative, perception is blocked. The perceptive person is an open person and a responsive person and hence a "caring" person. He or she is a person who is "in touch" with themselves and with others (people and nature). That person's part of the network of relations is alive and pulsing. In conclusion, I will share with you dilemmas experienced by two friends that manifest the "balance" in perceptiveness of impression and expression.

One friend was confronted with the reality of a totally free summer—three months without any demands or formal responsibilities. Before this time began he recognized both the possibilities and the dangers in this condition and took steps to deal with them. One danger was that of too much leisure, too much unscheduled time, and hence the possibility of boredom. He then planned his day in such a way that life would not just happen to him but also so that he would not be rigorously bound by a structured life. What does this have to do with perceptiveness beside the fact of my friend's recognition of his situation. I would suggest that by letting life happen, he saw that there would be too little input. In other words, he would become lazy and unreceptive. Without such input, his output would lessen. Thus he planned a "free schedule" in which perceptiveness was allowed to grow through both impression and expression.

Another friend is experiencing the opposite problem, too much input, too little leisure time. As a teacher, student, and single parent, she is continuously bombarded with input, with impressions to which she is called upon to respond. At the same time, she knows herself to be a person who does not have enough time to do all she wants to do and knows to be a part of herself. She knows that it is realistically impossible to express those aspects of herself. She then wonders if there is any way for her to be who she knows she is. This person is dealing with this dilemma by planning her life so that her perceptiveness might be a bit less "unbalanced." Hence, in the midst of the continual input and response, she keeps an eye open for moments of refreshment and revitalization. How she does this I will discuss further on in this present chapter.

Up to this point I have tried to confine myself to the operation of perceptiveness as impressive and expressive. Two elements intrinsic to perceptiveness were continuously in my mind and implicit in the above discussion, that is, sensitivity and awareness. In every discussion I have had about perceptiveness while in the process of writing this chapter these two words were central. I would ask a person what he or she thought was characteristic of a perceptive person. Almost universally and immediately, the response would include sensitivity and awareness. A perceptive person is a sensitive person, that is, a person whose senses are open and available to a great variety and subtleness of impressions and expressions. Such sensitivity is not necessarily accompanied by awareness or consciousness of what is sensed. If this is the case then sensitivity by itself is not yet perceptiveness. A perceptive person is a consciously sensitive person.

A Zen story may enable this idea about perceptiveness to become clearer. There was a blind man who lived near Bankei's temple. When Bankei died, the blind man told a friend: "Since I am blind, I cannot watch a person's face, so I must judge his character by the sound of his voice. Ordinarily when I hear someone congratulate another upon his happiness or success, I also hear a secret tone of envy. When condolence is expressed for the misfortune of another, I hear pleasure and satisfaction, as if the one condoling was really glad there was something left to gain in his own world. In all my experience, however, Bankei's voice was always sincere. Whenever he expressed happiness, I heard nothing but happiness, and whenever he expressed sorrow, sorrow was all I heard."[5] The focal point of this story is Bankei's purity of expression (his perceptiveness). I would also call attention to the perceptiveness of the blind man. His senses were keen. His discrimination was subtle. He was aware of what he sensed and could describe it. He was a consciously sensitive person, that is a perceptive person. Both the blind man and Bankei are "poor in spirit" in Meister Eckhart's under-

standing of this phrase: "To be poor in spirit is to be sensitive to other spirits."[6] Such sensitivity is conscious.

How can a person become perceptive? In general, I do
not believe that anyone is fully perceptive. Hence, growth
in perceptiveness is a lifelong task (at times a joy and at
other times a burden and even painful). However, perceptiveness is not only a task. It is also, to some extent, a given.
It is on this "given" quality of perceptiveness that I will first
focus. Each person is born into the world at a certain time,
in a certain place, within a particular culture and socio-
economic condition. Then the person is educated in accord with this culture and condition. Education is precisely
a training in perceptiveness, a schooling in conscious sensitivity. In fact, one of my friends would describe perceptiveness as "schooled observance." Such training applies
not only to the mind but also to the senses, for example, the
eye of a painter, the ear of a musician, the smell and taste
of a cook, the touch of a potter. Such schooling can be
"taken in" technically or/and creatively. Learning technically involves "taking in" a way to sense and an awareness
of this sense and then an imitating of the process exactly
until it becomes automatic. Creative learning involves "taking in" exactly the same "data" as in technical learning with
one major difference, that is, the use of this training to
further develop one's conscious sensitivity or perceptiveness. Merely technical learning can be a great advantage at
times, for example, when a person is without the physical
or emotional resources to operate at full. But, at the same
time, if a person is engaged only at the technical level, that
person can stagnate and become unperceptive and bound
into a systematic understanding of reality.

Perceptiveness can be lost or destroyed by sickness or
forgetfulness or ignorance or exhaustion. It is possible for

a person to care for their perceptiveness so that it will not be destroyed. Such care will also enable a person's perception to deepen and broaden, or, in a word, become more subtle. One of my friends is a teacher in a city high school. She is one of the few people I know who absolutely enjoys teaching in a high school. Many demands are made on her sensitivity. While in class, she is continuously trying to discover the moods and feelings and patterns of thought and insights of her students and then responds to what she discovers. An exhausting day! A few years ago, she and her husband decided to build a home away from the city. They bought a wooded property and designed their home to be part of this woods. One room in the home is her room. It has windows on three sides and can be used for work or relaxation or leisure. My friend describes her home as an aesthetic environment which she needs to give her own senses a time and a place to operate. I would also suggest that it is a place where she can care for her perceptiveness in terms of both its dimensions of impression and expression.

The care of perceptiveness, however, cannot depend on a person's socio-economic conditions. Another friend does not have the same financial resources as the person I just described. A few pages above, I spoke of a friend who had no leisure time and who wondered how she could be herself in the midst of constant demands on her perceptiveness. Her life is also exhausting. She continually studies her situation in its details, recognizes what she must do in terms of her commitments or duties and with respect to the question of where she is most needy. Once this area of neediness is uncovered, she asks what options are available to her. She then "tries on" the options mentally and/or actually in order to discover which one(s) are viable. Once this conclusion is reached, she structures or plans the viable options into her week. These options become sacred. For example, she will set aside a time to wash her hair once during the week; or try to read undisturbed or watch a lighted candle quietly in a dark room or listen to a record all the way through. The time and place for one or more of these options will be set up; everyone in her family is told about it. That time and place and option are sacred. Over the course of weeks or months, depending on the needs, the options will change. However, the general process of caring for her perceptiveness is carried out in an ongoing manner. She has made a conscious, planned decision and effort to become refreshed. The importance that I place on the two examples just described is not on what was and is done. This will be unique for each person. Rather, I went into detail to give expression to the importance of caring for one's perceptiveness. Such care is necessary for a person to continuously be consciously sensitive. It is not selfish or self-centered. It is rather manifestive of a concern for the network in which we live.

Perceptiveness is not only the result of training but is also spontaneous and zestful. (In the following chapter I will suggest that preceptiveness is also graceful. Thus, to say that it is the result of "training" is somewhat misleading.) A Hasidic story about Rabbi Moshe Leib begins to suggest what I mean here. One midnight the rabbi was absorbed in his mystical readings. He heard a rap on his window. A drunken peasant stood outside and asked for shelter and a bed for the night. For a moment the rabbi's heart was angry and he said to himself: "How can a drunk have the insolence to ask to be let in, and what business has he in this house?" But then he silently thought in his heart: "And what business has he in God's world? If God gets along with him can I reject him?" He opened the door at once and prepared a bed. The rabbi was spontaneous. It took him a moment to break out of his original interpretation of the situation and to perceive it with new eyes. A perceptive person is spontaneous insofar as the situation is perceived with a "beginner's mind," as if for the first time, with freshness. Yet, at the same time, the perception is grounded in training. The rabbi believed in God and this belief, nurtured by prayer and study, affected all his perceptions. Often a belief can confine a person's perceptiveness as happened initially to the rabbi who had a stereotype about drunks. That belief was challenged by his belief in God, and he then perceived the situation differently and spontaneously.

A second quality of a perceptive person is zest. A zestful person is a live person, a person who can taste the essence of a situation, can feel deeply the flavor of an impression or an expression. In the hands of a zestful person, a situation becomes alive. The network is animated. It is sensed and known. It becomes contagious.

A perceptive person is spontaneous and zestful. Such a person is not bound by the pattern of training or socialization undergone, but is able to make new connections and to savor them. This person is thoughtfully spontaneous and responsibly zestful. Jesus gave expression to this spirit when he declared that he had come that we might have life and have it to the full.

Furthermore, I would describe the preceptive person as an artist. By artist, I do not mean a person who can paint a portrait or landscape, or write a poem, or sculpt a madonna. Rather, I mean an "ordinary" person whose life is artistic. This person plunges into the everyday where we live and opens it up by word or silence, movement or stillness. A perceptive person lives life both artfully and artlessly.

In summary, perceptiveness is a human operation within the cosmotheandric network of relations by which a person can be "in touch" with the other elements and dimensions of the network. The operation involves impressions and expressions that are consciously sensitive. It is the way a person enters into the heart of the world. A prayerful person is a person who is open to that heart and in this openness touches upon the mystery that is God, the cosmos, and the human. Daniel Berrigan, while describing how the world confronted him with questions and refused to give him answers, wrote:

> Infinitely better than answers, the world showed me its heart. Slowly, subtly, with infinite compassion for my ignorance, it led me into the inner rhythms of human existence, the tides of fury and lust and fear and heartbreaking nobility which are its secret. I rode these tides. I learned (how slowly, with what resistance) that I was no priest until I consented, in those waters, to be a human being.[7]

Berrigan affirms a growth of perceptiveness, an unfolding of a secret. To pray is to search out that secret and to embrace it and then to be able to let it go in the further pursuit of the secret, the mystery. Such a prayer is the simple gaze at truth which Thomas Aquinas calls contemplation. Such a prayer is of the essence of sainthood, according to the Sufi, Hujwiri, who affirms that holiness "consists in seeing the things as they are—in being a seer."[8] To be a seer is to be able "to see," which is to be perceptive. And this is no easy task or condition for us to pursue,

> One of the boys at Nasrudin's school asked: "Which was the greatest achievement, that of the man who conquered an em-

pire, the man who could have but did not, or the man who prevented another from doing so?"

"I don't know about any of that," said Nasrudin, "but I do know a more difficult task than any of those."

"What is that?"

"Trying to teach you to see things as they really are."[9]

Notes

1. Paul Reps, *Zen Flesh, Zen Bones* (New York: Anchor), p. 3.
2. Martin Buber, *Tales of the Hasidim: The Early Masters* (New York: Schocken, 1947), p. 107.
3. Idries Shah, *The Pleasantries of the Incredible Mulla Nasrudin* (New York: Dutton, 1971), p. 13.
4. Bernard Lonergan, *Method in Theology* (New York: Herder and Herder, 1972), p. 59.
5. Paul Reps, *Zen Flesh, Zen Bones*, p. 30.
6. Raymond B. Blakney, trans., *Meister Eckhart* (New York: Harper Torchbook, 1941), p. 53.
7. Daniel Berrigan, *The World Showed Me Its Heart* (St. Louis, Missouri: National Sodality Service, 1966), p. 10.
8. Masaud Farzan, *The Tale of the Reed Pipe* (New York: Dutton, 1974), pp. 65–66.
9. Shah, *The Pleasantries of the Incredible Mulla Nasrudin*, p. 133.

8

Prayer as Grace

Persons who have attempted to develop their powers of perceptiveness and concentration can tell us that much hard work is involved. The same can be said for prayer. While this cannot be denied, it does not tell the whole story. For prayer is also grace, a gift. It happens when we least expect it to happen. When it does happen, there may be a feeling of having "let go." Prayer as the mystery of God and the world and humans coming to the surface cannot be merely conjured up at will. As St. Paul points out, no one can really say "Lord, Lord," unless he is moved by the Spirit of God. It is said from one's heart, which heart is the heart of the world, the Silence who is the Father—Abba. Prayer as grace is the grace that is realized in the midst of life. It involves the realization that I cannot control the responses or reactions to my words or actions by another. Nor do I entirely control my own responses and reactions. Not all depends on me. I can do what I am able or what I must do, but what happens involves the response of other people as well as the actualization of powers of which I am unaware. To live in a network of relations is to recognize that I am not self-sufficient.

A deep mystery is present in what is said above. It is a mystery that has wracked the minds and hearts of numerous people from many ages and cultures. It is the mystery of grace and effort.

A story is told in the gospel according to Mark about a woman who suffered with a hemorrhage for twelve years. She had undergone much painful treatment under a variety of doctors. Much effort had been expended for her cure. Everything had failed. This woman had heard about Jesus. One day she approached him with faith in her heart that she might be healed. She touched his clothes, believing that she would be cured. And the source of the bleeding dried up at that moment. This is grace.

Much effort is put into the tilling of the soil and the planting of a field. A farmer works to guarantee growth. He does all he can. But the growth is not entirely up to him. The weather is a part of the scene and the quality of the soil and many other factors which he cannot control. The farmer realizes the intimate connections of the network of relations. All the factors work for the growth of the seeds. This is grace.

A dancer strives for years to concentrate his or her energies, to develop form and movement. A time comes, possibly, when he or she seemingly dances without effort. The body flows in the rhythm of the music. It looks to us as if he or she does not strain at all. The dancer is graceful. This is grace.

"Think of the flowers; they never have to spin or weave. Yet, be assured, not even Solomon in all his regalia was robed like one of these. But you, you must not set your hearts on things to eat and things to drink; nor must you worry."[1] This passage may seem to be utterly fatalistic. Yet, it is quite expressive of grace. Each human person is unique. Each is precious. This is grace. The phrase, "nor must you worry," is also expressive of grace. Not to worry is not the same as being unconcerned nor does it mean that one does not plan. It simply points to the fact that neither the past, the present, nor the future are entirely the doing of one person or condition. Again, this is grace.

The interplay of grace and effort is also quite evident in friendship. There is nothing that one can do to guarantee the establishment of a friendship. I can work at a relationship and hope that it will develop into friendship. The working at the friendship is the effort. It is bringing myself to a relationship with whatever resources may be at my command and those that may spontaneously arise from my being. I cannot, however, determine the response of the other person. For me, this other's response is grace. I can trust another person. This trust may or may not lead to friendship. I cannot force another to trust me. Their trust of me is grace.

The interplay between grace and effort is developed in a unique manner in the Chinese attitude which is called *wei-wu-wei*, which can be translated as "doing without doing." Both elements are present here: effort is the "doing" and grace is the "not doing." The Chinese sage Chuang Tzu gives expression to this attitude:

Heaven does nothing: its nondoing is its serenity. Earth does nothing: its nondoing is its rest. From the union of these two nondoings all actions proceed, all things are made. How vast, how invisible this coming-to-be! All things come from nowhere! How vast, how invisible—no way to explain it! All beings in their perfection are born of nondoing. Hence, it is said: "Heaven and earth do nothing, yet there is nothing they do not do." Where is the man who can attain this nondoing?[2]

This man is the archer who when he shoots for nothing has all his skill. But when he shoots for a prize, his skill has not changed, but he himself is divided. He thinks more of winning than of shooting his bow.[3] To shoot demands effort. There is effort in "nondoing." There is also grace in "doing." When the effort is not divided, this is graceful effort. Again, this does not mean that there is no concern. To be concerned is to enter a situation with all the resources that are available. "Nondoing" is the allowing of the situation also to have its input. This is effortful grace, that is, when the effort of all involved is allowed to have play. Thus concern is also grace, my concern and your concern.

The integration of grace and effort is also very prominent in play. To play is to give oneself over to the game without being *overly* concerned about the outcome. To play is to give oneself to the game with all one's strength and skill and yet to lose oneself in it at the same time. The game has a structure, but not so much structure that we are bound or hemmed in. The structure, more or less, depends on the game. Its purpose is to allow the free play of one's strength and energies. These energies can become concentrated. Body and spirit can move with each other. They can "play into" each other. There is effort and there is grace. Prayer, especially worship or liturgy, may be compared to play. Liturgy is work, "work for the community," in its original Greek meaning. Yet, it is also a work in which people may lose themselves. When this liturgy arises from the Silence which is at its root, when it is expressive of the cosmotheandric network, it then becomes worship in spirit and in truth of which John the Evangelist speaks.[4] It is graceful.

Closely related to the playful aspect of gracefulness is its character of "flow." A recent psychological study suggests that activities are fun or rewarding in themselves because of their quality of "flow."[5] The image of "flow" reminds me of a river and its movement. The water is channeled by the banks of the river. These banks do not simply confine the water, but rather give it a structure for its movement, as do the rules of a game. The river moves smoothly. It flows. When this image is applied to human activity it points to the smoothness of that activity. A writer is said to flow when there is a smooth integration of his thought, feeling, and expression within the freeing structure of his language. A perceptive person flows when impression and expression are integrated. The cosmotheandric network of relations flows when the spaces and connections are respected and integrated. The opposite of "flow" is "awkward." Thus, at times, we meet up with "awkward" literary constructions. During the many weeks a child is learning to walk, the child's movement progresses from awkward to flow. After many more years the flow might become graceful, that is, flow without any awkwardness.

What makes flow to be flow? In a previous chapter, I spoke of finding the spaces in the network of relations. To flow is to move "in the spaces" without bumping into something or someone (both physically or psychologically). The person who flows is very aware and sensitive, that is, perceptive, yet such perceptiveness (in its awareness aspect) is not an obstacle to flow. It is an unself-conscious awareness. The awareness extends to the entire situation rather than to one's self alone. Thus unself-conscious awareness includes self-awareness not as isolated from the whole network, but as integrated within it. Flow is flow because of this kind of awareness which unself-consciously finds the spaces.

A person can be trained to flow, but such training does not necessarily result in flow. Flow is grace. Thus a person can be told the various movements necessary to swim. These movements can then be practiced with concentration for many hours. Suddenly, swimming becomes a joy. All the movements begin to work together with the water. The swimmer flows. The flow has taken effort but is finally the "result" of grace and effort. Another example is learning to ride a bicycle. A coordination of body movements with the bicycle joined with balance is striven for. After many attempts, balance is found. This is grace. The rider now flows. In both of these examples, the flow is related to the discovery of coordination. Imagine all the bodily muscles that must be coordinated in swimming or bicycle riding. We may be aware of some of these movements and make the effort to coordinate them. But we are never totally aware of all the movements. Once they all begin to work together, we begin to flow. Grace has happened.

Thus gracefulness involves "flow" which is an unselfconscious coordination of a person in themselves and between themselves and the other elements in the situation in which they are. Anne Morrow Lindbergh's suggestion about grace is close to this. She writes that "by grace I mean an inner harmony, essentially spiritual, which can be translated into an outward harmony."[6] I would add to this that not only is the harmony spiritual, but it is also natural. It is the diversity in unity of the cosmotheandric network.

Another aspect of grace is that it is unconditioned. It does not depend entirely on any one or any thing. It is lavish. The parable in Luke 15 of the gracious father gives expression to this dimension of grace. The father graciously welcomes his wandering son home. The father does not have to do this. The son had left with his inheritance. It is not necessary for the father to welcome him into his house again as a member of the household. But the father does welcome his son, and his welcome is not conditioned by any requirements. It is simply a gracious welcome. This grace is also called forgiveness. It involves a gratuitous lifting of the burden of the past from the shoulders of someone else or even from one's own shoulders; it involves a seeing that there is more than there appears to be—an unconditional acceptance of another or of oneself, the loving of another even when they are not understood. Here grace is not merely some thing. People are grace for other people.

All that has been said to this point about grace is prayerful. It may seem to be an impossible ideal. My point is that it is not an impossible ideal, but rather that it is a dimension of the very fabric of life. Life is effort and life is grace. Grace and effort are so interrelated in life that the very effort is graced.

The paradox of grace and effort is not solved. It cannot be solved as a mathematical equation. Rather, it is lived out in the changing life situations of each person. To pray is to be able to enter into these situations, into the network. Prayer is living these situations. In this way, it is of the essence of action and at the center of the active life. When lived, my action becomes my prayer and my prayer becomes my action. For, to "pray always"[7] as Paul tells us, is to live in the mystery we call life. Prayer involves the courage to meet each call from this cosmotheandric mystery.

Notes

1. Luke 12:27-29.
2. Thomas Merton, *The Way of Chuang Tzu* (New York: New Directions, 1965), pp. 101–102.

3. Ibid., p. 107.
4. John 4:23-24.
5. Cf. William B. Furlong, "The Fun in Fun," *Psychology Today* (June, 1976), pp. 35ff.
6. Anne Morrow Lindbergh, *Gift From the Sea* (New York: Pantheon, 1955), p. 23.
7. Cf. Ephesians 6:18-20.

9

Prayer as Wisdom

In the previous chapters we have viewed a variety of the human roots of the experience of prayer in questioning, wonder, silence, concentration, preceptiveness, and grace. Each of these experiences is grounded in the fertile soil of the cosmotheandric network of relations. In this final chapter, I would like to suggest that the intrinsic connection among these experiences is wisdom, and that the search for and expression of wisdom is prayer. In the Book of Wisdom we read that the spirit of the Lord is wisdom and that this spirit is "that which holds all things together."[1] We read further that wisdom is "an inexhaustible treasure to men, and those who acquire it win God's friendship."[2] The acquisition of wisdom is the realization of the divine dimension of the network of relations and is the way to the realization of that dimension. Wisdom is the "goal" and the means to the "goal." Prayer is the term and the way to the term. The term and the goal, the way and the means are identified in the cosmotheandric network.

What is wisdom? Wisdom is often associated with age—the wise old man or woman. However, wisdom is not restricted to the elderly. It can also be found in the young. It is my present task to attempt a description of wisdom. In general, I cannot adequately describe wisdom. For wisdom, like prayer, can only be pointed to. It cannot be defined. In the chapter on speaking about prayer I referred to a story about Duke Hwan of Khi and the wheelwright. The wheelwright spoke of the wisdom found in books as the dirt that the sages have left behind. The ancient wise people took their wisdom to the grave with them. What they left behind—the words—is merely dirt. That dirt, however, may be enlivened. It can become fertile soil. It itself may not be wisdom. But it may be able to point us to wisdom. This can happen when the words are taken to heart, when the words are taken into the reader and become part of that reader, when the words come alive again in a living, pulsing person. These words sometimes speak to a heart that is open to them because those words are the words which fit exactly into a situation. It is then that wisdom is born. Elie Wiesel suggests this when he writes:

> Sometimes it happens that we travel for a long time knowing that we have made the long journey solely to pronounce a certain word, a certain phrase, in a certain place. The meeting of the place and the word is a rare accomplishment on the scale of humanity.[3]

This meeting is wisdom.

Many words have been spoken in the praise of wisdom. They have been written in the Jewish and Christian scriptures and in the sacred writings of the Orient. Today, often, wisdom is relegated to the oriental guru. We forget that the teacher in Israel is a wise person. We forget that Jesus "grew in wisdom before God and man." In what does the wisdom of these sages consist? Where can it be found?

While wisdom, like prayer, is a gift, it also comes from instruction and association with the wise. Wise persons arise in all the various religions as well as outside of formal religion. I will first speak of some of these wise persons and then I will attempt to point to the nature of wisdom based on the lives of these persons. At the same time I will be speaking of prayer. The wise person is a prayerful person.

In the gospel according to Luke we read that Jesus grew in wisdom and knowledge and love before God and man.[4] St. Paul speaks of the Christ as the wisdom of God.[5] With all the talk about Jesus as God or as human, as savior or redeemer, it is easy to forget that he is a wise person. What is it about Jesus that manifests his wisdom? He himself rarely speaks of wisdom. Only a few of his followers are presented in the gospels as disciples of a sage. Thus to discern his wisdom it is necessary to seek it in his manner of living. This style I would broadly categorize as wisely compassionate. It comes through to the reader of the gospels in the various attitudes of Jesus toward the many people he met.

Often Jesus was invited to dinner with the leaders of the town through which he was passing. One time he was invited to a meal in the home of a pharisee called Simon. While at table, a woman entered the room and went to Jesus and began to wash his feet with her tears and to dry them with her hair. Simon objected because of the bad reputation of the woman. Jesus responded with a parable which pointed to the heart of the situation:

> There was once a creditor who had two men in his debt; one owed him five hundred denarii, the other fifty. They were unable to pay, so he pardoned them both. Which of them will love him more?[6]

The pharisee responded to the question of Jesus by pointing out that the one who had been forgiven more would

love more. Jesus confirmed this response. He did not con-
demn the pharisee but rather attempted to allow him to
come to an awareness of the fundamental issues involved,
to perceive the heart of the situation in which he partici-
pated. This is wisdom.

There were also many times when Jesus was questioned
by people whom he met. At times the questions were attempts to trick him. His responses were often such that the
question was thrown back at the inquirer in such a way that
the one questioning was confronted with his or her own
question in regard to his or her own life. An obvious
example of this is the dialogue between Jesus and the leaders in regard to the woman taken in adultery.[7] The same
happened when a lawyer asked Jesus: "Who is my
neighbor?" Jesus responded with the parable of the Good
Samaritan and concluded by turning the question back to
the lawyer. The real question is not, "Who is my
neighbor?" but "To whom are you a neighbor?"[8] A final
example of the wisdom and compassion of Jesus that I will
suggest is the delightful story of Zacchaeus. Zacchaeus was
a tax collector and hence not well received by the people
from whom he collected the taxes. He had heard that Jesus
would pass near his home. So, he climbed a tree to get a
better look. When Jesus saw him, he saw into his heart and
asked if he could dine with this lowly tax collector rather
than with the leaders of the town. Appearances and reputation did not cloud the perception of Jesus. He saw beyond them to the heart of the person.[9] This is of the essence of wisdom.

Another illustration of the way of wisdom is found in the
life of the Buddha, the Enlightened One. Oriental art pre-
sents us with many pictures of the Buddha. He is repre-
sented as a man of wisdom or of compassion or of both.

This spirit is well illustrated in a story told of his attitude to many speculative questions that he was asked. A disciple of the Buddha once wondered if the world was eternal or not eternal. He asked the Buddha to enlighten him. The Buddha responded with the following parable:

> It is as if a man had been wounded by an arrow thickly smeared with poison and his friends and companions, his relatives and kinsfolk, were to procure for him a physician or surgeon; and the sick man were to say: "I will not have this arrow taken out until I have learnt whether the man who wounded me belonged to the warrior caste, or to the Brahmin caste, or to the agricultural caste, or to the menial caste."
>
> Or again he were to say, "I will not have this arrow taken out until I have learnt the name of the man who wounded me, and to what clan he belongs."
>
> Or again he were to say, "I will not have this arrow taken out until I have learned whether the man who wounded me was tall, or short, or of the middle height."
>
> Or again he were to say, "I will not have this arrow taken out until I have learnt whether the man who wounded me was black, or dusky, or of a yellow skin. . . ."
>
> That man would die without ever having learnt the answers to his questions.
>
> In exactly the same way any one who should say "I will not follow the Buddha until he explains to me either that the world is eternal or that the world is not eternal," that person would die.
>
> For whether the world is eternal or not eternal, there still remain birth, old age, death, sorrow, lamentation, misery, grief, and despair. My concern is the cure of these maladies.[10]

The questions to which the Buddha will respond, the concerns for which he will show a care are those that arise from the very life of the person. The Buddha is filled with a compassion for the suffering person. He has an eye for that which is truly suffering and that which is truly a cure. This is wisdom.

A third example of a wise person is found in the founder of Hasidism, the Baal-Shem-Tov, the Master of the Good Name of God. The following story is illustrative of the spirit of this wise Jewish man. It speaks not only of his wisdom but also of a way to discern if a person is wise or not:

> The disciples of the Baal-Shem heard that a certain man had a great reputation for learning. Some of them wanted to go to him and find out what he had to teach. The master gave them permission to go, but first they asked him: "And how shall we be able to tell whether he is a true zaddik (wise person)?" The Baal-Shem replied: "Ask him to advise you what to do to keep unholy thoughts from disturbing you in your prayers and studies. If he gives you advice, then you will know that he belongs to those who are of no account. For this is the service of men in the world to the very hour of their death; to struggle time after time with the extraneous, and time after time to uplift and fit it into the nature of the Divine Name."[11]

This is wisdom, to see into the heart of the everyday, each day. It is not necessarily a single answer. Nor does it mean a different answer all the time. Rather, it is to meet the everyday, to struggle with it, and seeing into its heart, to uplift it, and to be uplifted.

Wisdom often arises out of a question and leads to another question, the latter question probing the life of the inquirer. Wisdom gathers what is scattered as it scatters what is thought to be gathered. It is deeply compassionate and leads to wonder and silence. It is expressive of a sage's intrinsic relatedness to a particular situation, yet places that unique event in the context of Mystery. To be wise is to see things as they are. And this is prayer. Finally, wisdom is a gift. It is grace. St. Paul speaks of this gift when he writes:

> How rich are the depths of God—how deep his wisdom and knowledge—and how impossible to penetrate his motives or understand his methods! Who could ever know the mind of the Lord? Who could ever give him anything or lend him anything? All that exists comes from him; all is by him and for him. To him be glory forever! Amen.[12]

To pray is to search out the mind of God, to attempt to penetrate his motives and methods and ways. To pray is to do this in the midst of life, in the midst of our questionings and wonderings and silences. To pray is to seek out the mystery in the heart of life, to see things as they are, to be perceptive in the midst of our relations. To pray involves a seeing into the heart of life, with compassion and understanding, knowledge and love. It does not shrink from action, but acts when action is called for and remains quiet when quiet is demanded. To pray is to live!

Notes

1. Wisdom 1:7.
2. Wisdom 7:14.
3. Elie Wiesel, *The Town Beyond the Wall* (New York: Avon, 1969), p. 118.
4. Luke 2:52.
5. 1 Corinthians 1:24.
6. Luke 7:41–42.
7. Cf. John 8:1–11.

8. Cf. Luke 10:29–37.

9. Luke 19:1–10.

10. E. A. Burtt, ed., *The Teachings of the Compassionate Buddha* (New York: Mentor, 1955), pp. 34–35.

11. Martin Buber, *Tales of the Hasidim: The Early Masters* (New York: Schocken, 1947), p. 66.

12. Romans 11:33–36.

Conclusion

These pages have been about prayer. It might have seemed that I had wandered many times away from my subject. Traditionally, prayer has been spoken of as prayer of petition, praise, thanksgiving, and reparation. It has been described as contemplation. I have not used this language because I believe that it can be misleading. It is a language that often relegates prayer to a chapel or to a formalized setting. This formal prayer, whether it is in written forms, or whether it is spoken in one's own words; whether it is in the quiet of one's room or chapel; whether it is shared prayer, is not exactly what I have been speaking of. It is not excluded. But it is seen to be too narrow a description. I have been trying to uncover various experiences that are at the root of such prayer and to which such prayer can lead. My thesis is that participation in such root experiences is itself prayerful.

It is my experience that prayer happens in the day to day, and that the formulations we generally associate with prayer are expressions of various dimensions of this everyday. As I see it, that everyday is a cosmotheandric network of relations, a network in which three dimensions are intricately woven: the divine, the human, and the cosmic. Within this network we question and wonder and are silent. We try to see our relations in this network as clearly as possible, with sensitivity and awareness and compassion. We, in a word, seek wisdom, the flavor of life at the heart of life. To be engaged in these experiences is to pray.

The very fiber of life is prayer. While we may learn to pray at a time and in a place, prayer happens at no special time, in no special place. Prayer is grace. Its limits are the boundaries of human existence itself, which boundaries can be described as mystery, the "evermore" of life.

Where is that mystery? Right here, right now. And we can see and hear and touch it with our bodies and our minds and our hearts. Yet, at the same time it can be missed. I will conclude with some free verse which gives expression to my experience of prayer, an experience which itself sometimes touches the heart and sometimes misses.

PRAYER?

To enter a dark room
The sun has shone here
It is warm
I do not know the sun
It is here—I know
I know it not

To be in a dark room
Reaching for walls that
never appear
I do not know them
They are here—I know
I know them not

To serve in a dark room
To love in a dark room

To open my eyes in a dark room
To pain in a dark room
To be available in a dark room
To be tired in a dark room
To be controlled in a dark room
To control in a dark room
To be alienated in a dark room
To be finite in a dark room
To be scared in a dark room
To rejoice in a dark room
To listen in a dark room
To work in a dark room
To see in a dark room
To walk in a dark room
To stumble in a dark room
To fall in a dark room
To sleep in a dark room
To get up in a dark room

To ask nothing
To receive nothing
To possess nothing

To ask everything
To receive everything
To possess everything

Sometimes. . .